GAMBLING AND C

Gambling and Gaming Licensing

A Practical Guide

Roger Butterfield

Shaw & Sons

Published by
Shaw & Sons Limited
Shaway House
21 Bourne Park
Bourne Road
Crayford
Kent DA1 4BZ

www.shaws.co.uk

© Shaw & Sons Limited 2008

Published June 2008

ISBN 978 0 7219 1720 7

A CIP catalogue record for this book is
available from the British Library

Printed in Great Britain by
Athenæum Press Limited, Gateshead

CONTENTS

Contents

FOREWORD

Gambling and betting – age-old customs enjoyed even by the ancient civilisations of China, Egypt and Rome – have throughout much of history avoided legislation and regulation. In the UK, laws to regulate their practice were only introduced, for the first time, in the last century, despite the fact that horseracing has been taking place regularly here since the twelfth century!

The Gambling Act 2005, which came into effect in late 2007, is a necessary overhaul of the outdated 1968 legislation of gaming and betting. The new Act significantly updates the UK's existing gambling laws, introducing new structures of protection for children and vulnerable adults, as well as bringing the burgeoning Internet gaming sector into British regulation for the first time. The legislation transfers responsibility for licensing gambling from magistrates to Licensing Authorities. Furthermore, the Act introduces a new, unified regulator for gambling in Great Britain – the Gambling Commission – and a new licensing regime for commercial gambling (operated and regulated by the Commission or by Licensing Authorities, depending on what is being licensed). A two-tier system of licensing is introduced for certain gambling operations: for example, betting shops and casinos now require an operating licence from the Gambling Commission and also a premises licence from the Licensing Authority.

The above changes have wide-reaching consequences, affecting casinos, betting shops, bingo halls, amusement arcades, pubs and clubs with gaming machines, and small lotteries. This book explains the purpose of the legislation, how applications have to be made, the procedures to be followed by Licensing Authorities, what conditions can be attached to licences, the differences between operating licences, personal licences and premises licences, the objectives of the legislation and the enforcement of the law as it relates to gambling. It is hoped that it will provide a clear, easy-to-use guide through the complex procedures of the 2005 Act.

Roger Butterfield

TABLE OF STATUTORY INSTRUMENTS

Part 1
INTRODUCTION

PURPOSE OF THE LEGISLATION

The Gambling Act 1968 was nearly 40 years old when the new legislation, the Gambling Act 2005, came into force in September 2007. Since the implementation of the original Act, there have been many changes in the way gambling is provided and offered.

The Gambling Act 2005 is intended to bring the law regulating gambling up-to-date.

Underpinning the legislation are the three licensing objectives:

1. To prevent gambling being a source of, or associated with, crime and disorder.

2. To ensure that gambling is conducted in a fair and open way.

3. To protect children and other vulnerable persons from being harmed or exploited by gambling.

Section 335 of the Gambling Act 2005 enables contracts entered into in connection with gambling to be legally enforced in the courts.

Throughout the text of this book, unqualified references to section numbers refer to the Gambling Act 2005.

TYPES OF LICENCE

The Gambling Commission issues operating licences and personal licences. Once the appropriate licences have been obtained from the Commission, a premises licence is required from the Licensing Authority before the premises can be opened.

Operating licence

An operating licence is a licence which states that it authorises the licensee:

(a) to operate a casino (a "casino operating licence");

(b) to provide facilities for playing bingo (a "bingo operating licence");

(c) to provide facilities for betting other than pool betting (a "general betting operating licence");

(d) to provide facilities for pool betting (a "pool betting operating licence");

(e) to act as a betting intermediary (a "betting intermediary operating licence");

(f) to make gambling machines available for use in an adult gaming centre (a "gaming machine general licence" for an adult gaming centre);

(g) to make gaming machines available for use in a family entertainment centre (a "gaming machine general licence" for a family entertainment centre);

(h) to manufacture, supply, install, adapt, maintain or repair a gaming machine, or a part of a gaming machine, within one of Categories A to D (a "gaming machine technical operating licence");

(i)   to manufacture, supply, install or adapt gambling software ("gambling software licence"); or

(j)   to promote a lottery (a "lottery operating licence") (section 65).

Section 67 will require a "remote operating licence" for remote gambling.

An operating licence cannot be issued for both remote and non-remote gambling. However, the Gambling Commission can issue operating licences which cover more than one of the ten kinds of licence, provided the activities are all either remote or non-remote.

Personal licence

Under section 127, a personal licence is a licence which authorises an individual to perform the functions of a specified management office or to perform a specified operational function in connection with:

(a)   the provision of facilities for gambling; or

(b)   a person who provides facilities for gambling.

Under section 80, the Gambling Commission is able to attach conditions to operating licences to ensure that in respect of each such licence at least one person:

(a)   occupies a specified management office in or in respect of the licensee or in connection with the licensed activities; and

(b)   holds a personal licence authorising the performance of the functions of the office.

"Management office" in relation to a licensee means:

(a)   if the licensee is a company, the office of a director;

(b)   if the licensee is a partnership (including a limited liability partnership), the office of a partner;

(c)   if the licensee is an unincorporated association, any office in the association; and

(d)   in any case, any position the occupier of which is required, by the terms of his appointment, to take or share responsibility for:

   (i)   the conduct of a person who performs an operational function in connection with a licensed activity; or

   (ii) facilitating or ensuring compliance with terms of conditions of the operating licence.

"Operational function" means:

(a)   any function which enables the person exercising it to influence the outcome of gambling;

(b)   receiving or paying money in connection with gambling; and

(c)   manufacturing, supplying, installing, maintaining or repairing a gaming machine.

Small scale operator

Anyone holding an operating licence must have at least one person in a management office holding a personal licence. Section 129, however, exempts small scale operators from this requirement. This is because, in the small scale operations, the operating licence will achieve the same purpose as a personal licence.

Definition of small scale operator

The Gambling Act 2005 (Definition of Small Scale Operator) Regulations 2006 define "small scale operator".

For the purposes of section 129 of the Gambling Act 2005,

and subject to Regulation 3 of the Regulations, a small scale operator is the holder of an operating licence (the licensed activity):

(a)   where there are no more than three qualifying positions in or in respect of the licensee or in connection with the licensed activity; and

(b)   each qualifying position is occupied by a qualified person.

"Qualifying position" means a position which is held by a person who, by the terms of his appointment, has primary responsibility for:

(a)   the management of the licensed activity;

(b)   the management of the financial affairs of the licensee;

(c)   ensuring the licensee complies with the requirements of the Act;

(d)   the marketing of the licensed activity;

(e)   the management of the information technology facilities used in the provision of the licensed activity;

(f)   the management of the licensed activity for a particular locality or area in Great Britain in which there are situated five or more sets of premises in respect of each of which the licensee holds a premises licence; or

(g)   the management of a single set of premises in respect of which a casino or bingo premises licence has effect.

"Qualified person" means a person who is:

(a)   named on the operating licence as a person who holds a qualifying position; or

(b)   the subject of an application to vary the operating licence under section 104(1)(b) of the Act (application to vary licence) to add his name as a person holding a qualifying position, and:

    (i)   the application complies with sections 69(2)(g)(a)(fee)and104(5)(accompanying statement) of the Act; and

    (ii)   the application has not been withdrawn or finally determined.

Premises licence

A premises licence is a licence which states that it authorises premises to be used for:

(a)   the operation of a casino (a "casino premises licence");

(b)   the provision of facilities for the playing of bingo (a "bingo premises licence");

(c)   making Category B gaming machines available for use (an "adult gaming centre premises licence");

(d)   making Category C gaming machines available for use (a "family entertainment centre premises licence"); or

(e)   the provision of facilities for betting, whether by making or accepting bets or by acting as a betting intermediary (a "betting premises licence").

A casino premises licence is:

(a)   a "regional casino premises licence" if it relates to a regional casino;

(b)   a "large casino premises licence" if it relates to a large casino; and

(c)   a "small casino premises licence" if it relates to a small casino.

A premises licence must:

(a)   specify the name of the person to whom it is issued;

(b)   specify a home or business address of that person;

(c)   specify the premises to which it relates;

(d)   specify the activities for which it authorises the premises to be used;

(e)   specify any conditions attached by the Licensing Authority;

(f)   specify any default conditions which have been excluded by the Licensing Authority;

(g)   include a plan; and

(h)   if a period for the life of a licence is specified, specify the period the licence will last.

There may only be one premises licence in force at a time for the premises covered by that licence. However, section 152 of the Act provides that, in respect of track betting, there may be more than one premises licence in force but one premises licence can operate only in respect of one specific part of the overall premises.

In such a case, there is a main betting premises licence for the track and other premises licences for the additional gambling activities can be granted. On race days, children and young persons are able to enter the betting part of the premises where bets can be placed.

Licensing Authorities must maintain a register of premises licences to be available for public inspection. The content of the register is prescribed in regulations.

Applications for premises licences can be made by individuals, companies or partnerships. Before an application can be made for a premises licence, they must have a legal right to occupy the premises. In addition, they must have been granted an operating licence or have made an application for one. The Licensing Authority cannot issue the premises licence until an operating licence has been granted. The only exception is in respect of a premises licence for betting at tracks where an operating licence is not required.

LICENSING OBJECTIVES

Under section 1 of the Gambling Act 2005 the licensing objectives are:

(a) preventing gambling from being a source of crime or disorder, being associated with crime or disorder or being used to support crime;

(b) ensuring that gambling is conducted in a fair and open way; and

(c) protecting children and other vulnerable persons from being harmed or exploited by gambling.

When applications are made for operating licences, the applicant has to address how the three licensing objectives will be met. For example, this could include steps that they will take to ensure their staff are suitable; action that they will take if they consider that the proceeds of crime may be being laundered through gambling; steps that will be taken to ensure people below 18 do not get into premises or parts of premises where they should not be and what action the staff will be trained to take if they believe that someone below the age of 18 is present.

Applicants for premises licences do not have to address the objectives on the application form. However, in certain cases, e.g. bingo premises licenses and family entertainment centre premises licences, there will be mandatory conditions regarding the location and supervision of machines that no-one below the age of 18 years can play.

Part 2
OPERATING AND PERSONAL LICENCES

APPLICATIONS FOR OPERATING LICENCES

Applications for operating licences have to be submitted on the statutory form. If any false information is provided, or information that should have been revealed is not supplied, an offence will be committed under section 342 of the Gambling Act 2005.

The form must contain information about the primary contact; the name of the operator; the type of organisation, e.g. partnership, corporate body; where the head office is located; the type of operating licence being applied for; and then full details of all the premises currently used, together with details of directors, partners, senior managers and above who are responsible for the ongoing operation of the business. Full details have to be provided about any investigation that has been carried out by any statutory or government body, together with details of any convictions or police cautions, reprimands or warnings that have been issued either in the United Kingdom or abroad. A business plan and annual report or audited accounts must also be provided. In addition, an independent financial adviser must verify that the applicant has sufficient funds to support the proposed activities for the next two years.

Operators must show how they have procedures to ensure that all equipment used for gambling complies with the Commission's technical standards. In addition, applicants have to address the three licensing objectives and show that they have procedures to ensure gambling is conducted in a fair and open way, procedures to ensure children and other vulnerable persons will be protected from being harmed or exploited by gambling and procedures to ensure that the business is protected from being a source of, or being associated with, any criminal activities and to prevent criminal activities taking place in or around the premises including money laundering, drug misuse and disorderly behaviour.

FEES FOR OPERATING LICENCES

The fees for operating licences are set out in the Gambling (Operating Licence and Single-Machine Permit Fees) Regulations 2006 as amended by the Gambling (Operating Licence and Single-Machine Permit Fees) (Amendment) Regulations 2007.

The level of fees to be paid depends upon the nature of the operation. In respect of general betting operating licences, the fee to be paid depends on the number of premises operated by the applicant. The same principle applies in respect of operating licences for adult gaming centres and family entertainment centres. Schedule 1 to the 2006 Regulations sets out the various categories of non-remote operating licences and sets out the bands that will determine what level of fees are paid.

There is an annual fee payable for an operating licence and this must be paid within 30 days of the date on which the operating licence was issued.

APPLICATIONS FOR PERSONAL LICENCES

Anyone who requires a personal licence must apply on the prescribed form. Applicants will have to provide documentary evidence to satisfy the Gambling Commission of their identity. They will also have to provide two photographs.

The application form requires full information about an applicant's identity, including whether or not they have been known by any other name, e.g. aliases, maiden name. Home addresses for the previous five years must be provided. The applicant then has to indicate whether or not they are applying for a personal management licence or a personal functional licence and then indicate the sector they will be working in. The employer of the applicant must then confirm their identity and confirm they have certified the criminal bureau check carried out by the applicant.

If the applicant is a member of a professional body, e.g. The Law Society, this information must be provided, as must details of any civil legal action taken against the applicant in the last five years. Full details of employment experience and academic qualifications must be provided, as must full details of the financial circumstances of the applicant and their partner/spouse. Applicants must then confirm whether or not they have been found guilty of a relevant criminal offence or accepted a formal police caution, reprimand or warning, either in the United Kingdom or abroad, or if they are currently subject to any criminal investigation or pending prosecution.

There are two categories of personal licences – personal management licences and personal functional licences. Personal management licences are for people like directors and area managers. Personal functional licences are currently only required for staff working in casinos. This includes the staff working on the tables and also people providing door security services.

GAMBLING APPEALS TRIBUNAL

If an application for an operating licence or a personal licence is refused, or conditions are attached to the operating licence which the applicant does not like, they can appeal to the Gambling Appeals Tribunal. There is also a right of appeal to the tribunal against action taken by the Gambling Commission during the currency of a licence, e.g. attaching extra conditions and/or revoking a licence. The composition of the Tribunal is the President and other members of the Tribunal, all of whom are appointed by the Lord Chancellor. A person may only be a member of the Tribunal if they are legally qualified.

Under section 144 of the Gambling Act 2005, the Appeal Tribunal can confirm the decision of the Gambling Commission, substitute any decision that the Commission could have made, quash the Commission's decision in whole or in part or add to the Commission's decision. They can also send the matter back to the Commission for a determination in accordance with a finding made by the Tribunal or a direction given by them.

Under section 142 of the Gambling Act 2005, the time for bringing an appeal to the Gambling Appeals Tribunal is "before the end of the period of one month beginning with the date of the decision appealed against". However, under section 142(2), the Tribunal may permit an appeal to be instituted after the end of that period.

Section 145 provides that a decision by the Gambling Commission has no effect while an appeal to the Gambling Appeal Tribunal (a) could have been brought, or (b) has been brought but is not finally determined or abandoned.

The Gambling Appeals Tribunal Rules 2006 set out the procedure to be followed when lodging an appeal and the steps to be taken by the Tribunal after an appeal is lodged.

The Rules regulate the procedure for appeals to the Gambling Appeals Tribunal and are set out as follows.

Part 1 (Rules 1 to 3) introduces the Rules and includes interpretation of terms used in the Rules.

Part 2 (Rules 4 to 20) contains preliminary matters, which take place prior to the appeal hearing.

Part 3 (Rules 21 to 29) applies when the appeal hearing has commenced.

Part 4 (Rules 30 to 32) makes provision for appeals from the Tribunal to the High Court in England and Wales or, in Scotland, the Court of Session.

Part 5 (Rules 33 to 42) makes provision for general matters such as the register kept by the Tribunal and the Rules that apply to the sending of notices.

In particular, the Rules make the following provisions.

1.   Rule 4 provides for the bringing of an appeal by the appellant filing an appeal notice with the Tribunal.

2.   Rule 5 provides that a statement of case must be filed by the Commission in support of its determination and Rule 6 provides that the appellant must reply to that statement of case. Both Rules set out the information that the relevant documents should contain and also state that they should be accompanied by a list and copies of certain information, all of which must be filed with the Tribunal.

3.   Rule 8(2) allows a party to request that a document that they are otherwise obliged to disclose is exempted from such disclosure on the grounds that it would not be in the public interest, that the document contains commercially sensitive information, that the document is privileged or that it is disproportionate to the case to order such disclosure.

4. The direction-making powers of the Tribunal are contained in Rules 10 to 13 and 15 and 16. Rule 10 provides that the Tribunal may make directions to ensure the just, expeditious and economical determination of the appeal. Rule 11 lists examples of particular directions that the Tribunal may give; Rules 12, 13, 15 and 16 provide further information about the making of a particular direction listed in Rule 11.

5. Rule 18 applies where the Tribunal directs that a hearing to determine a preliminary question of law or fact is to take place before the substantive hearing of the appeal takes place.

6. Rule 20 applies where the Tribunal directs that a pre-hearing review of the case is to be held. The purpose of a pre-hearing review is to assist the Tribunal in ensuring the fair and prompt hearing of the appeal by making any directions necessary to achieve that objective.

7. Rule 21 applies when the Tribunal determines an appeal without an oral hearing. When an appeal is determined in accordance with this Rule, the Tribunal must consider whether it is undesirable to publish the whole or part of its final determination. The Tribunal will take into account the circumstances of the case, such as whether there are matters of commercial sensitivity or personal details relating to key personnel in an organisation or relating to a personal licence holder before deciding to publish the whole or part of its final determination.

8. Rule 22 provides an exemption to the general rule that all hearings must be held in public. The Tribunal will look at the particular circumstances of the case and will allow the hearing to take place without the attendance of the press and public when it considers that it is in the interests of justice to do so. Under this Rule, the Tribunal can

permit any other person to attend a private hearing when it thinks that it is necessary for the fair hearing of the appeal; for example, the attendance of an interpreter.

9. Rule 27 allows the Tribunal to consider whether it would be undesirable to publish the whole of its final determination when the whole or part of the hearing was held in private.

10. Rule 28 allows the Tribunal to make a costs order against the appellant or the Commission in relation to the bringing of the appeal or their conduct.

11. Rules 30 and 31 apply when a person seeks permission from the Tribunal to bring an appeal against the final determination of the Tribunal to the High Court in England and Wales or the Court of Session in Scotland. The application for permission to bring an appeal in these circumstances must be decided without an oral hearing, unless the Tribunal considers that a hearing is desirable.

In accordance with the Gambling Appeals Tribunal Fees Regulations 2006, fees are payable for lodging appeals unless the appellant is in receipt of qualifying benefit, or they are in receipt of an income-based job seekers allowance or a guarantee credit under the State Pension Credit Act 2005. Qualifying benefit is income support or working tax credits provided that the gross annual income for the calculation of the working tax credits is £15,460 or less.

The Tribunal has discretion to waive or reduce a fee if payment would involve undue financial hardship. In addition, under Regulation 5, if the fee has been paid at any time when it should not have been paid, the fee shall be refunded. An appellant wanting a refund of the fee should apply in writing within six months of paying it but the Tribunal may extend this period if there is a good reason for the application being made later than the six months.

Part 1 – fees payable

On filing an appeal of a description set out in Part 2 (opposite) in relation to one of the operating licences listed:	*Fee (£)*
Casino operating licence in accordance with section 65(2)(a)	13,070
Bingo operating licence in accordance with section 65(2)(b)	2,905
General betting operating licence in accordance with section 65(2)(c)	9,335
Pool betting operating licence in accordance with section 65(2)(d)	9,335
Betting intermediary operating licence in accordance with section 65(2)(e)	9,335
Gaming machine general operating licence for an adult gaming centre in accordance with section 65(2)(f)	1,450
Gaming machine general operating licence for a family entertainment centre in accordance with section 65(2)(g)	1,450
Gaming machine technical operating licence in accordance with section 65(2)(h)	1,450
Gambling software operating licence in accordance with section 65(2)(i)	1,450
Lottery operating licence in accordance with section 65(2)(j)	8,710
On filing an appeal of a description set out in Part 2 (opposite) in relation to one of the personal licences listed:	
Personal management licence in accordance with sections 127 and 80(5)	1,450
Personal functional licence in accordance with sections 127 and 80(6)	755
Voiced bet order	
On filing an appeal under section 337(1) against the Gambling Commission's order under section 336(1) to void a bet	8,710

Part 2 – appeals for which fees are payable

* An appeal under section 141(1) against the Gambling Commission's decision not to issue or renew an operating or personal licence.

* An appeal under section 141(2) against the Gambling Commission's decision to attach a condition to an operating or personal licence.

* An appeal under section 141(3) against the Gambling Commission's decision that an operating licence shall not continue to have effect when there is a new company controller.

* An appeal under section 141(4) against the Gambling Commission's decision to refuse to vary an operating or personal licence following an application to vary under section 104.

* An appeal under section 141(5) against the Commission's notification relating to the lapse of an operating or personal licence due to mental or physical incapacity.

* An appeal under section 141(6) against the Gambling Commission's exercise of a section 117 regulatory power to:

    (i)   give warning
    (ii) attach an additional condition to a licence
    (iii) remove or amend a condition attached to a licence
    (iv) make, amend or remove an exclusion to a remote licence under section 67(1)
    (v)   suspend a licence
    (vi) revoke a licence
    (vii) impose a penalty

* An appeal under section 141(7) against the Gambling Commission's decision to suspend a licence, except following a section 116 review.

* An appeal under section 141(8) against the Gambling Commission's decision to revoke a licence, except following a section 116 review.

* An appeal under section 141(9) against the Gambling Commission's decision to impose a penalty under section 121.

REVIEW BY THE GAMBLING COMMISSION

The Commission may conduct a general review as to the manner in which licensees in a particular sector are carrying on licensed activities (section 116(1)). In addition, the Commission has the power under section 116(2) to review an individual licence if:

(a)   there is reason to suspect that activities may have been carried on in purported reliance on the licence but not in accordance with a condition;

(b)   the Commission believes that the licensee, or a person who exercises a function in connection with the licensed activities, has acquired a conviction of a specified kind; or

(c)   for any reason the Commission:

    (i)   suspects that the licensee may be unsuitable to carry on the licensed activities; or

    (ii)   thinks that a review would be appropriate.

On completion of a review the Commission may:

(a)   give a warning;

(b)   attach an additional condition to the licence;

(c)   remove or amend a condition already attached to the licence;

(d)   make, amend or remove an exclusion on the licence;

(e)   suspend the licence;

(f)   revoke the licence;

(g)   impose a financial penalty.

When dealing with reviews, the Commission will initially consider whether or not there should be a criminal investigation or a regulatory enquiry. The indications are that, if the Commission considers a regulatory investigation is the appropriate route to follow, it will not normally consider criminal proceedings. This decision may be reviewed, however, if it is established during the investigation that information provided has been false or deliberately misleading.

SPECIFIC REGULATORY REVIEW PROCESS

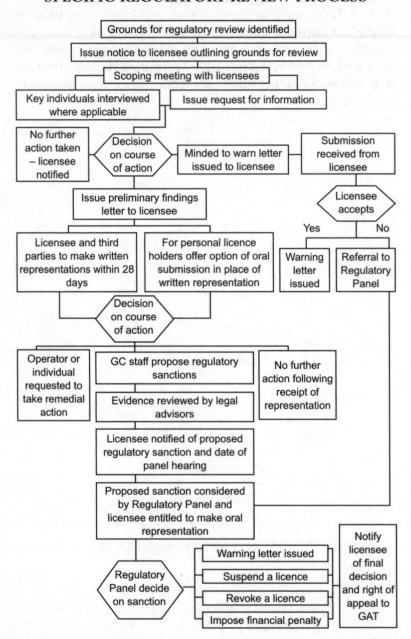

EXEMPTIONS

Private gaming and betting

There is an exemption in paragraphs 1, 3, 4 and 5 of Schedule 15 to the 2005 Act for people who provide facilities for private gaming. The exemption applies as long as the gaming is equal chance gaming and in private, i.e. a place where the public do not have access and there is no charge for admission.

Paragraphs 2 and 4 of Schedule 15 remove the need for the gaming to be equal chance gaming where the gaming is residential or domestic. This applies where the gaming takes place in a private dwelling (domestic) and where the activity takes place in a hostel, hall of residence or similar and more than half the participants are residents (residential).

Non-commercial gaming and betting

Non-commercial gaming is defined as gaming which takes place at a non-commercial event, i.e. an event where none of the money raised after the amounts expended in respect of prizes or other costs reasonably incurred in organising the event have been deducted is used for private gain. If these conditions are complied with, the gaming is exempt under the Gambling Act 2005. An example where this exemption would apply is a charity having a race night to raise funds. The person providing the films could be paid, prizes could be provided and then the balance of the money goes to the good cause.

Certain conditions must be observed for the exemption to apply:

- The people attending must be told where the profit from the event is going.

- Arrangements must be in place to ensure that the profits are applied for a purpose other than private gain.

- The event does not take place on premises holding a premises licence or temporary use notice.

- There is no remote gambling.

GAMING MACHINES

Categories of Machine

The main provisions on gaming machines can be found in Part 10 of the Gambling Act 2005.

Section 235 defines a gaming machine as a machine which is designed or adapted for use by individuals to gamble (whether or not it can also be used for other purposes). Section 235(5) contains a power to provide for circumstances in which a single piece of apparatus which is a gaming machine is to be treated as more than one gaming machine. Regulation 2 of the Gaming Machine (Single Apparatus) Regulations 2007 provides that, if a gaming machine is available for use to more than one person at a time, then it is to be treated as the number of gaming machines equal to the number of people able to use it at that time, e.g. a machine where two people can play together is to be regarded as two machines.

Section 235(2) exempts equipment which is not regarded as gaming machines such as home computers, machines for betting on real future events, machines which sell lottery tickets provided that the results of the lottery are not determined by the machine, and machines designed or adapted for the playing of bingo where the machine is used under a permit or gaming machine operating licence.

The Secretary of State has the power to define by regulations four classes of gaming machine known as Categories A to D. In addition to dividing Category B into sub-categories, regulations defining the categories may provide for:

(a) the maximum stakes payable for use of the machine;

(b) the value or nature of the prize delivered as a result of its use; or

(c) the types of premises on which it can be used.

The current regulations are the Categories of Gaming

Machine Regulations 2007, the Gambling Act 2005 (Gaming Machines) (Definitions) Regulations 2007 and the Gaming Machine (Circumstances of Use) Regulations 2007.

Category A machines

Category A machines can only be installed in a regional casino. There is no limit on the amount of money that can be staked or the amount of the prizes. The Gambling Act 2005 imposes a limit of one regional casino; however, for the time being, the Government have announced that this will not be allowed.

Category B machines

Category B is divided into five categories.

1.   A Category B1 machine can only be installed in casinos. The size of the casino will determine the number of machines that can be installed.

2.   B2 machines are fixed odds betting terminals. They can be installed in casinos and betting shops.

3.   B3A machines are lottery machines. These can only be installed in clubs or miners' welfare institutes with a club gaming permit or club machine permit.

4.   B3 machines can be installed in casinos, betting shops, bingo premises and adult gaming centres.

5.   B4 machines can be installed in the same premises as B3 machines. In addition, three B3 machines can be installed in clubs or miners' welfare institutes holding the appropriate permit.

The B3A machines (lottery machines) have no connection with the National Lottery. The law that relates to the National Lottery, i.e. people over 16 may take part, does not apply to B3A machines and the provisions of the Gambling Act 2005 apply (no-one under the age of 18 may play B3A machines).

Category C machines

Category C machines replace the previous section 34(5E) permits. The machines can be installed in bingo premises with no limit, adult gaming centres with no limit, family entertainment centres with a premises licence with no limit and, if they wish, clubs and public houses.

Category D machines

Category D gaming machines are the only ones that can be played by people below the age of 18 years. They can be installed in any premises which are permitted either by a licence or a permit to have gaming machines.

Notices

Category A, B and C machines will have to bear a notice stating that no-one below the age of 18 can play the machines. In addition, a notice will have to be displayed giving the telephone number of Gam-care or a similar organisation and a notice giving the percentage pay out of the machine or where this information can be found.

Summary of restrictions on machines and premises

The table below shows the stake and prize limits on each category of machine.

Machine Category	Maximum stake	Maximum prize
A	Unlimited	Unlimited
B1	£2	£4,000
B2	£100	£500
B3A – Lottery machine	£1	£500
B3	£1	£500
B4	£1	£250
C	50p	£35
D	10p or 30p when non-monetary prize	£5 cash or £8 non-monetary prize

Reading the Act and the Regulations together, the following table sets out what machines can be installed where, and how many:

Premises type	A	B1	B2	B3	B4	C	D
			Machine Category				
Regional casino (table/machine ratio of 25:1 up to maximum)	Maximum of 1,250 machines comprising any combination of machines in Categories A to D within the total limit of 1,250 (subject to table ratio)						
Large casino (table/machine ratio of 5:1 up to maximum)		Maximum of 150 machines comprising any combination of machines in Categories B to D within the total limit of 150 (subject to table ratio)					
Small casino (table/machine ratio of 2:1 up to maximum)		Maximum of 80 machines comprising any combination of machines in Categories B to D within the total limit of 80 (subject to table ratio)					
Pre-2005 Act casinos (no table/machine ratio)		Maximum of 20 machines, Categories B to D, or C to D machines instead					
Betting premises and tracks occupied by pool betting			Maximum of 4 machines in Categories B2 to D				
Bingo premises				Maximum of 4 machines in Category B3 or B4		No limit on Category C or D machines	
Adult gaming centre				Maximum of 4 machines in Category B3 or B4		No limit on Category C or D machines	
Family entertainment centre (with premises licence)						No limit on Category C or D machines	

	Machine Category						
Premises type	A	B1	B2	B3	B4	C	D
Family entertainment centre (with permit)							No limit on Category D machines
Clubs or miners' welfare institutes with permits					Maximum of 3 machines in Categories B3A, B4 to D		
Qualifying alcohol licensed premises						1 or 2 machines of Category C or D, automatic upon notification	
Qualifying alcohol licensed premises with gaming machine permit						Number as specified on permit	
Travelling fair							No limit on Category D machines

PUBLIC HOUSES AND OTHER LICENSED PREMISES

Section 281 of the Gambling Act 2005 enables premises holding an on-premises licence for the sale of alcohol issued under the Licensing Act 2003 to have an automatic entitlement to two gaming machines of Category C or D. To take the benefit of this entitlement, the holder of the premises licence under the 2003 Act must notify the Licensing Authority of their intention to make two machines available. A prescribed fee of £50 will have to be paid (the Gaming Machines in Alcohol Licensed Premises (Notification Fee) (England and Wales) Regulations 2007). In addition, any code of practice regarding the supervision and operation of the machines must be complied with (section 282(3)).

A public house that installs gaming machines must comply with the Gambling Commission Code of Practice. It is a condition that:

1. All gaming machines are located in a place so that their use can be supervised, either by staff whose duties include such supervision, by other means (e.g. CCTV), or both.

2. Arrangements must be in place for such supervision.

3. All gaming machines must be in a place that requires a customer who wants to use any ATM machine in the premises to cease gambling to use the ATM machine.

The Code also sets out the following best practice guidelines:

1. Procedures should be put in place to prevent underage gambling, including for:

    (a) checking the age of apparently underage customers;

    (b) refusing access to anyone who appears to be underage and who tries to use a Category C machine and cannot produce an acceptable form of identification.

2. Reasonable steps should be taken to ensure all relevant employees understand their responsibilities to prevent underage gambling, e.g. training of staff and keeping records of training.

3. The only acceptable proof of identification must:

   (a) contain a photograph from which the individual can be identified;

   (b) be valid; and

   (c) be legible and have no visible signs of tampering or reproduction.

   Acceptable forms of identification include Citizencard, Connexions card, driving licence and passport.

4. Procedures should be in place for dealing with cases where a child or young person repeatedly attempts to gamble on a Category C machine in a public house: the matter should be reported to the Gambling Commission and the police and information on problem gambling be made available.

If a public house fails to comply with the Code, the Licensing Authority can take action, e.g. cancel the permit, vary the number and/or Category of machines or take away the right to have machines at all.

If the operator of a public house wishes to install more than two machines, they may do so by applying for a licensed premises gaming machine permit (section 283). The fees for licensed premises gaming machine permits are prescribed in the Gambling Act 2005 (Licensed Premises Gaming Machine Permits) (England and Wales) Regulations 2007. If a public house had more than two machines on 31 August 2007, they do not need to apply for a licensed premises gaming machine permit until their current authorisation expires. The fee in this case is £100 for the permit. However, if a public house only has two machines and wishes to increase the number to exceed two machines or the public house wishes to install machines for the first time and have more than two, the fee is £150. In addition, there is an annual fee of £50.

Under Schedule 13 to the Gambling Act 2005, the Licensing Authority must prescribe the form and manner in which applications are made for licensed premises gaming machine permits. Licensing Authorities may require the application to be served on the Authority and the police, or the Authority, the police and the Gambling Commission. In addition, the Authority could require the application to be advertised.

The Licensing Authority can grant an application for the permit, refuse it, or grant it for a smaller number of machines or a different category of machines from those requested, or both (Sch 13, para (2)).

There is no power to attach a condition to a permit (Sch 13, para 5(1)).

The Licensing Authority can cancel or vary a licensed premises gaming machine permit (Sch 13, para 16(1)). Before cancelling or varying a permit, the Authority must give the permit holder 21 days' notice of their intention and hold a hearing if the holder of the permit requests one (Sch 13, para 16(2)).

An application can be made for the transfer of a licensed premises gaming machine permit if the applicant is applying for the transfer of the on-premises licence.

The Licensing Authority must maintain a register of licensed premises gaming machine permits issued by them and make arrangements for the register to be available for public inspection at all reasonable times (Sch 13, para 22(1)).

Gaming in public houses

Provided relevant regulations are complied with, public houses can allow customers to play certain games.

The Gambling Act 2005 (Exempt Gaming in Alcohol-Licensed Premises) Regulations 2007 prescribe the maximum amounts that may be staked and won in equal chance games provided in premises with an on-premises alcohol licence issued under the Licensing Act 2003.

	With no permit	*With licensed premises gaming machine permit*
Equal chance gaming	Yes	Yes
Unequal chance gaming	No	No
Stake and prize limits	Maximum of: (1) £5 per person per game (all types of gaming) (2) £100 per day (poker only) Maximum prize in any game of poker is £100 No maximum stake for games of dominoes and cribbage	Maximum of: (1) £5 per person per game (all types of gaming) (2) £100 per day (poker only) Maximum prize in any game of poker is £100 No maximum stake for games of dominoes and cribbage
Participation fee	No	No
Deductions or levies	No	No
Gaming machines	Category C and/or D – maximum of two machines, subject to notification to the Licensing Authority	Category C and/or D – as many machines as approved by the Licensing Authority and specified in the permit

FAMILY ENTERTAINMENT CENTRE GAMING MACHINE PERMIT

Family entertainment centre permits allow gaming machines to be provided without an operating or premises licence. These premises are often referred to as unlicensed family entertainment centres. The permits are issued by Licensing Authorities under the procedure in Schedule 10 to the Act and authorise the use of the lowest category machine in places which do not have a gambling premises licence or alcohol licence.

A family entertainment centre is defined as premises (other than an adult gaming centre) wholly or mainly used for making gaming machines available for use. Only Category D machines can be installed at premises operating with a family entertainment centre gaming machine permit.

The Licensing Authority may grant an application for a family entertainment centre permit only if they are satisfied that the applicant occupies or proposes to occupy the premises and intends to use the premises as an unlicensed family entertainment centre (Sch 12, para 2). A Licensing Authority may not attach conditions to a family entertainment centre permit and cannot restrict the number of machines operated under a permit (Sch 10, para 8).

The Licensing Authority will have to prescribe the application form and the manner in which the application should be made and specify what other information and documents, e.g. insurance certificates and plans, they require to accompany the application (Sch 10, para 5).

When exercising their functions under Schedule 10, a Licensing Authority may (but need not) have regard to the licensing objectives but must have regard to any guidance issued by the Gambling Commission.

Unless a family entertainment centre permit has been

surrendered, lapsed or forfeited, it will normally last for ten years.

When a family entertainment centre applies for renewal of its permit, the application may only be refused if access to the centre has been refused without reasonable excuse or renewal would not be reasonably consistent with pursuit of the licensing objectives (Sch 10, para 18(4)).

The application for renewal must be submitted not more than six and not less than two months before the expiry date. There is no provision for late renewal on the grounds of inadvertence (Sch 10, para 18).

There is no provision for cancellation of a family entertainment centre permit. Such a permit cannot be transferred; the new occupier of the premises must apply for a further permit.

Appeals from decisions of a Licensing Authority in relation to family entertainment centre permits may be made to the magistrates' court.

The Authority may prepare a statement of principles that they propose to apply when considering applications for family entertainment centre permits. In particular, they may want to set out the matters that will be taken into account in determining the suitability of the applicant (Sch 10, para 7). This could include requiring applicants to provide Criminal Record Bureau checks; information regarding staffing levels; a list of checks that will be carried out on applicants for jobs at the premises; their opening hours; and whether there will be a minimum entry age for unaccompanied children.

An application for a permit may be granted only if the Authority is satisfied that the premises will be used as an unlicensed family entertainment centre and if the police have been consulted on the application. Relevant considerations to take into account would be the applicant's suitability, e.g. have they any convictions, and the suitability of the premises in relation to their location and any issues about disorder.

A permit may lapse:

(a)   if the holder ceases to occupy the premises (Sch 10, para 13);

(b)   if the Licensing Authority notifies the holder that the premises are not being used as an unlicensed entertainment centre (Sch 10, para 14);

(c)   if an individual permit holder dies, becomes incapable by reason of mental or physical incapacity, becomes bankrupt, or sequestration of his estate is ordered (Sch 10, para 15(1)); or

(d)   if the company holding the permit ceases to exist or goes into liquidation (Sch 10, para 15(2)).

The permit must be kept on the premises (Sch 10, para 19) and it is an offence not to produce it when requested by a constable, enforcement officer or authorised person (Sch 10, para 20).

Where the holder of a permit is convicted of a relevant offence as set out in Schedule 7 to the Gambling Act 2005, the court can order forfeiture of the permit (Sch 10, para 17).

A Licensing Authority must maintain a register of permits issued by them. This register is available for inspection by the public who are entitled to a copy of any entry in the register, subject to a reasonable fee being paid (Sch 10, para 23).

The fee payable for a family entertainment centre gaming machine permit is prescribed in the Gambling Act 2005 (Family Entertainment Centre Gaming Machine) (Permits) Regulations 2007.

CLUB GAMING PERMITS/CLUB MACHINE PERMITS

The Act provides for members' clubs and miners' welfare institutes, but not commercial clubs, to apply to the Licensing Authority for a gaming permit.

Commercial clubs, as well as members' clubs and miners' welfare institutes, may apply for a club machine permit.

Club gaming permits and club machine permits allow the provision of no more than three gaming machines from Categories B3A, B4, C or D, except that commercial clubs cannot install B3A machines.

In respect of gaming machines, the Act stipulates that:

(a) no child or young person uses a Category B or C machine in the premises;

(b) the holder complies with any relevant provision of a code of practice about the location and operation of gaming machines;

(c) machines can only be used by members of the club and their guests (section 273(3)).

A club gaming permit also allows the club to provide facilities for gambling, provided the gambling meets the following conditions in respect of games of chance:

(a) the games are prescribed in regulations – Pontoon and Chemin de Fer;

(b) no participation fee is charged otherwise than in accordance with regulations – the maximum fee is £3 (the Gambling Act 2005 (Club Gaming Permits) (Authorised Gaming) Regulations 2007);

(c) no amount is deducted from sums staked or

won otherwise than in accordance with the regulations;

(d)   children and young persons are excluded from any area of the premises where the gaming is taking place (section 271).

A club machine permit authorises the provision of gaming machines but does not authorise the provision of any other type of gaming facility. However, the Gambling Act 2005 (Exempt Gaming in Clubs) Regulations 2007 allow clubs with a permit to allow their patrons to play certain games as long as the financial limits prescribed in the regulations are complied with.

Procedure

Applications will be made to the Licensing Authority on the form prescribed in regulations. Within seven days beginning on the date on which the application is made, the applicant must also send a copy of the application to the Gambling Commission and the police. Those two parties may object to an application for a permit, although such objections must be lodged within 28 days beginning on the date on which the application was made to the Licensing Authority. If an objection is made, two copies of the objection must be sent to the Authority setting out reasons for the objection (the Gambling Act 2005 (Club Gaming and Club Machine Permits) Regulations 2007).

The Licensing Authority may grant or refuse the application. The limited grounds of refusal are as follows:

1.   The applicant does not fulfil the requirements for a member's club, commercial club or miner's welfare institute.

2.   The applicant's premises are used wholly or mainly by children or young people.

3. An offence under the Act or a breach of permit has been committed by the applicant while providing gaming facilities.

4. A permit held by the applicant has been cancelled in the previous ten years.

5. An objection has been lodged by the Commission or the police (Sch 12, para 6).

If the Authority is satisfied on either of the first two grounds, they must refuse the application. In deciding whether to grant a permit in the remaining three circumstances, the Authority must have regard to any relevant guidance issued by the Gambling Commission, and the licensing objectives.

A club gaming permit and club machine permit are, by virtue of section 271 and section 274, subject to three mandatory conditions:

1. Persons may only use gaming machines if they have been members of the club or institute, or applied or were nominated for membership, at least 48 hours before use, or are the guests of such a person.

2. No person under 18 years of age shall use a Category B or C machine.

3. The holder of the permit must comply with any relevant Gambling Commission Code of Practice about the location and operation of gaming machines.

A Licensing Authority has no discretion to attach any other conditions to either type of permit (Sch 12, para 8(2)).

A fast track procedure is provided for clubs or institutes which hold a club premises certificate under section 72 of the Licensing Act 2003 to apply for a club gaming permit or club machine permit. There is no opportunity for objections to be made by the Gambling Commission or police and the fast track procedure reduces the grounds on which a Licensing Authority can refuse a permit (Sch 12, para 10). The fee to be paid for a fast track application is £100. In the event of a new club opening and applying for a permit, the fee is £200. An annual fee of £50 is payable.

There does not seem to be a time limit after which the fast track procedure cannot be used. A club holding a certificate under section 72 of the Licensing Act 2003 could apply at any time for a club gaming permit or club machine permit to take advantage of the fast track procedure. This would enable a club, opening after the Gambling Act 2005 came into force and obtaining a certificate under section 72, to apply for a permit under the fast track procedure.

Subject to one exception, club permits last for ten years (Sch 12, para 17). A permit granted under the fast track procedure to a club with a club premises certificate will last indefinitely (Sch 12, para 17). An annual fee is payable in respect of club permits (Sch 12, para 14).

Application for renewal must be made not more than three months or less than six weeks before expiry. There is no provision for late renewal on the grounds of inadvertence (Sch 12, para 24).

The Licensing Authority may cancel a permit if:

(a)   premises are used wholly by children and/or young persons; or

(b)   an offence has been committed under the Gambling Act 2005; or

(c)   breach of a permit condition has been committed in the course of gaming activities by a permit holder (Sch 12, para 21).

Appeals may be made to the magistrates' court from Licensing Authority decisions relating to club gaming and club machine permits by the following:

(a)   a club or institute following rejection of its application;

(b)   the Gambling Commission or police if they unsuccessfully opposed the grant of a permit;

(c)   a permit holder following cancellation of the permit (Sch 12, para 25).

Exempt gaming in clubs

Section 269 of the Gambling Act 2005 authorises members' clubs, commercial clubs and miners' welfare institutes to provide facilities for equal chance gaming without the need to obtain any further authorisation under the 2005 Act, providing they comply with conditions laid down in the Act and Regulations. The Gambling Act 2005 (Exempt Gaming in Clubs) Regulations 2007 prescribes the financial limits that must be complied with to enable clubs to benefit from the statutory provisions.

Under Regulation 2 of the 2007 Regulations, a club is able to provide poker as long as the maximum stake per person per game does not exceed £10, the maximum amount staked on games of poker in any one day does not exceed £250 and the total amount staked on all games of poker held in the club in any period of seven days does not exceed £1,000. Regulation 3 provides that the maximum prize that can be won in any game of poker is £250.

If a club does not hold a club gaming permit under Regulation 4, the maximum participation fee that a club can charge for a person to take part in any game is £1 or, in the case of a commercial club that holds a club machine permit, £3. The only exception to this is in respect of bridge or whist, where a club may charge a participation fee of £18 if the game is played on a day on which no facilities for other kinds of gaming, other than bridge or whist, are being provided by the club.

Where a club gaming permit is held, a club may charge people £20 to participate in games of bridge or whist, if the game is played on a day on which no facilities for any kind of gaming, other than bridge or whist, are being provided. In respect of other games of equal chance, a club holding a club gaming permit may charge a maximum of £3.

Clubs established for gaming

Sections 266(1) and 267(1) of the 2005 Act provide that a club which is established or conducted wholly or mainly for the purposes of providing facilities for gaming does not qualify as a members' club or a commercial club. This means they could not apply for a club gaming permit or a club machine permit. However, under the legislation, the Secretary of State can make regulations prescribing certain types of gaming that would enable a club established wholly or mainly for the purposes of providing facilities for gaming to apply for a permit. The Gambling Act 2005 (Gaming in Clubs) Regulations 2007 provide that a club established or conducted to provide bridge or whist can be a members' club or a commercial club and be able to apply for a permit.

As previously mentioned, paragraph 10 of Schedule 12 to the 2005 Act provides that, if the club holds a club premises certificate under section 72 of the Licensing Act 2003, they are entitled to a fast track application for a club gaming or club machine permit. However, a Licensing Authority does not have to grant an application if they think the applicant is established or conducted wholly or mainly for the purposes of the provision of facilities for gaming other than bridge or whist.

The types of games that may be played in clubs and the financial limits are shown in the table opposite.

	Members' club, commercial club or institute (with no permit)	Members' club or institute (with club gaming permit)	Members' or commercial gaming club (with no permit)	Members' gaming club (with club gaming permit)	Members' club, commercial club or institute (with club machine permit)
Equal chance gaming	Yes	Yes	Yes	Bridge and/or whist only	Yes
Banker's or unequal chance	No	Pontoon/Chemin de Fer	No	No	No
Stake and prize limits	Poker: £1,000 per week, £250 per day, £10pp per game Other gaming: none, but expectation that it should be for low stakes	None	Poker: £1,000 per week, £250 per day, £10pp per game Other gaming: none, but expectation that it should be for low stakes	None	Poker: £1,000 per week, £250 per day, £10pp per game Other gaming: none, but expectation that it should be for low stakes
Maximum participation fees	Bridge and/or whist: £18pp Other gaming: £1pp	Bridge and/or whist: £20pp Other gaming: £3pp	Bridge and/or whist: £18pp Other gaming: £1pp	£20 per person	Bridge and/or whist: £18pp Other gaming: £3pp
Levies or deductions from stakes or prizes	No	No	No	No	No
Gaming machines	No	Up to 3 Category B3A, B4, C or D	No	Up to 3 Category B3A, B4, C or D	Up to 3 Category B3A, B4, C or D

All clubs holding either club gaming permits or club machine permits must comply with the Gaming Machine Permits Code of Practice.

Conditions on club gaming permits and club machine permits are as follows:

1. All gaming machines must be located in a place within the premises where they can be supervised either by staff whose duties incude such supervision (including bar staff or floor staff) or by other means, e.g. CCTV.

2. The club must have in place arrangements for such supervision.

3. All machines must be located in a place that requires any customer who wishes to use a cash machine available on the premises to stop gambling before they can use the cash machine.

Failure to comply with any of the above could result in the Licensing Authority considering revoking the permit.

It is considered best practice for clubs with permits to:

1. Put into effect procedures to prevent underage gambling, including checking the age of apparently underage customers and refusing access to anyone who appears underage and who tries to use a Category B or C machine and cannot produce an acceptable form of identification.

2. Take all reasonable steps to ensure all relevant employees understand their responsibilities for preventing underage gambling, e.g. training of staff.

3. Instruct staff that the only acceptable identification must:

    (a) contain a photograph from which the individual can be identified;

    (b) be valid;

    (c) be legible and have no visible signs of tampering or reproduction.

4.   Have procedures in place for dealing with cases where a child or young person repeatedly attempts to gamble on Category B or C machines, including oral warnings, reporting the offence to the Gambling Commission and the police, and making available information on problem gambling.

One of the licensing objectives is the protection of vulnerable persons. The Code recommends that clubs holding either of the permits should put in place procedures for encouraging a person who may be gambling more than they should, gambling beyond their means or who cannot make informed or balanced decisions about gambling because of mental impairment, alcohol or drugs to exclude themselves from the club. In addition, the club should take all reasonable steps to refuse service or to otherwise prevent an individual who has entered into a self-exclusion agreement from participating in gambling.

Clubs that have introduced a system of self-exclusion should put in place procedures to ensure an individual who has self- excluded cannot gain access to gambling. The system should include:

(a)   a register of those excluded and relevant details, e.g. name, address, membership number or account details held;

(b)   photo identification (where available and in particular where enforcement of the system may depend on photographic identification) and a signature;

(c)   staff training to ensure that relevant staff are able to enforce the system; and

(d)   the removal of those self-excluded persons found in the gambling area or attempting to gamble from the premises.

Self-exclusion procedures should require the individuals involved to take positive action, e.g. a signature on a self-exclusion form.

Before a person makes the decision to self-exclude, the club should provide or make available (e.g. by leaflets providing telephone numbers of organisations that can assist people who may be addicted to gambling) sufficient information about what the consequences are of self-exclusion.

Clubs should take all reasonable steps to ensure that:

1. Self-exclusion is for a minimum of six months and give customers the option of extending this to a total of at least five years.

2. A customer who has decided to enter into a self-exclusion agreement is given the opportunity to do so immediately without any cooling-off period. However, if the customer wishes to consider the self-exclusion further (e.g. with Gamblers Anonymous or Gam Care) the customer may return at a later date to sign the self-exclusion form.

3. At the end of the period chosen by the customer (and at least six months later), the self-exclusion remains in place unless the customer takes positive action in order to gamble again. No marketing material may be sent to the individual unless he has taken positive action in order to gamble again and has agreed to accept such material.

4. Where a customer chooses not to renew, and makes a positive request to begin gambling again, the customer is given one day to cool off before being allowed access to gambling facilities.

It is not expected that the club will carry out an assessment or make any judgement of whether the individual should have access to gambling. The requirement to take positive action in person or over the phone is purely to:

    (a) check that the customer has considered the decision to gain access to gambling again and allow them to consider the implications; and

(b)   implement the one-day cooling-off period and explain why this has been put in place.

To assist with preventing underage gambling, under the Code of Practice for equal chance gaming in clubs and public houses the club must appoint a gambling supervisor. That person must put into effect procedures designed to prevent underage gambling including:

(a)   holding gaming in parts of the club which are restricted to adults;

(b)   checking the age of any potentially underage players; and

(c)   refusing access to anyone apparently underage who cannot produce acceptable proof of age identification.

The supervisor must take reasonable steps to ensure all employees are aware of their responsibilities under the Code.

Procedures should be in place for dealing with cases where an underage person repeatedly attempts to gamble, including verbal warnings and reporting the matter to the police and the Gambling Commission.

Where equal chance gaming is taking place in clubs, before the game starts:

1.   All payments should be made in cash.

2.   All players should be notified of any stake limits that apply.

3.   All equipment used in gaming should be supplied by the premises.

In respect of poker the supervisor must keep a record of:

(a)   the number of games played;

(b)   the number of players; and

(c)   the amount staked.

BINGO

Bingo operating licence

Section 91 enables the Secretary of State to make regulations attaching conditions to bingo operating licences. These include the power to limit the amount of stakes or participation fees or value of prizes; or requiring a specified proportion of stakes to be paid out by way of prizes; or imposing requirements specific to bingo games that are played on more than one set of premises.

No-one under 18 may be employed in bingo premises if they are involved in providing any facilities for gambling. Children under 16 cannot be employed in any capacity at any time when facilities for playing bingo are being offered. However, young persons aged 16 and 17 may be employed in bingo premises, while bingo is being played, provided the activities on which they are employed are not connected with the gaming or gaming machines.

Premises holding a bingo premises licence will be able to make available for use up to four Category B3 or B4 machines and any number of Category C and D machines.

Children and young persons under 18 can go into premises holding a bingo premises licence. They cannot play bingo but could play a Category D machine if such machines were installed in the bingo hall. A notice must be displayed at a prominent place at every entrance to the bingo hall stating that no-one under the age of 18 is permitted to play bingo (Sch 2, para 1, Gambling Act 2005 (Mandatory and Default Conditions) (England and Wales) Regulations 2007).

Where a bingo hall does allow children and young persons into the premises, there is a mandatory condition which attaches to all bingo premises licences that requires Category B and C machines to be in an area that is separated from the remainder of the premises by a physical barrier which is effective to prevent access other than by an entrance designed for that purpose. The entrance must be supervised at all times to ensure that children or young persons do not enter the area, and the area must be so arranged that all parts of it can be supervised by the member or members of staff who have responsibility for ensuring children or young persons do not enter the area or by the staff who have responsibility for monitoring the area by CCTV (Sch 2, para 3, Gambling Act 2005 (Mandatory and Default Conditions) (England and Wales) 2007).

Bingo in clubs and public houses

Bingo can be played in public houses and clubs with no authorisation needed under the Gambling Act 2005, unless the bingo offered is a "high turnover bingo". When that is the case, a bingo operating licence and a bingo premises licence are required. The key element as to whether or not bingo is "high turnover bingo" is whether or not the total stakes or prizes for bingo games played in any seven-day period exceed £2,000. Once the stakes or prizes have exceeded £2,000, a "high turnover" period begins. The "high turnover" period expires at the end of the year beginning with the first day of the seven-day period that caused the high turnover period to begin. A period of seven days any of which is in a high turnover period does not cause a new high turnover period to begin.

Under section 275, the licensee of the public house or the club must inform the Gambling Commission if at any time its bingo becomes high turnover bingo. If during the next twelve months "high turnover bingo" takes place and the public house or club has not obtained an operating licence and a premises licence, an offence will have been committed.

PRIZE GAMING

Gaming is prize gaming if the nature and size of the prize is not determined by the number of people playing or the amount paid for or raised by gaming, e.g. playing bingo at the seaside.

A prize gaming permit is a permit issued by the Licensing Authority to authorise the provision of facilities for gaming with prizes on specified premises.

Certain premises can offer prize gaming without a prize gaming permit:

1. Casinos can offer any form of prize gaming, other than bingo. A casino operating licence will give authority to provide all games of chance except any form of bingo. A casino could obtain a bingo operating licence if it wished to do so.

2. Prize gaming can be provided on bingo premises. The bingo operating licence allows bingo operators to provide prize gaming in respect of equal games of chance (section 291).

3. Any type of prize gaming may be provided in adult gaming centres and licensed family entertainment centres. Unlicensed family entertainment centres may offer equal chance prize gaming under the auspices of their gaming machine permit without the need for a prize gaming permit (section 290).

4. Travelling fairs are able to offer equal chance prize gaming without a permit provided that the facilities for gambling, including Category D machines, are an ancillary amusement at the fair (section 292).

Children and young persons may participate in equal chance prize gaming only.

Section 293 of the Act sets out four conditions that permit holders, adult gaming centres, family entertainment centres and travelling fairs must comply with to lawfully offer prize gaming. The conditions are:

1. They must comply with the level of fees as set out in regulations.

2. All chances to take part in the gaming must be allocated on the premises on which the gaming is taking place and on one day, the game must be played and completed in the day the chances are allocated and the result of the game must be made public in the premises on the day it is played.

3. The prize for which the game is played must not exceed the amount set out in regulations.

4. Participation in the gaming must not entitle the player to take part in any other gaming (section 293).

Prize gaming permits

Any other premises that wish to offer prize gaming must apply for a prize gaming permit. The application can only be made by a person who occupies or plans to occupy the premises. An application cannot be made for a permit if a premises licence or a club gaming permit is in effect for the same premises (Sch 14, para 5).

The Licensing Authority must specify the form and manner in which the application should be made and specify what information they require to be submitted with the application (Sch 14, para 6).

The Licensing Authority may prepare a statement of the principles they propose to apply when considering applications for prize gaming permits. In particular, they may want to set out the matters that they will take into account in determining the suitability of the applicant.

The Licensing Authority can grant or refuse an application for a prize gaming permit but cannot add conditions (Sch 14, para 9). The Authority can only grant a permit if they have consulted the police about the application (Sch 14, para 10). Relevant considerations to take into account would be the suitability of the applicant, including any convictions, and the suitability of the premises in relation to their location and issues about disorder.

Prize gaming permits are subject to conditions that:

(a)   any levels of fees and prizes set out in regulations are complied with;

(b)   all games must be played entirely in one day and the result of the games must be made public (section 293).

A permit cannot be issued in respect of a vehicle or a vessel.

A prize gaming permit will last for ten years and there is no annual fee payable (Sch 14, para 13).

If the holder of a prize gaming permit is convicted of a relevant offence, the court may order the forfeiture of the permit (Sch 14, para 17).

The Licensing Authority must maintain a register of permits issued under Schedule 14. It is a public register and members of the public are entitled to a copy of entries in the register, subject to paying a reasonable fee (Sch 14, para 23).

The fees for equal chance prize gaming permits are prescribed by the Gambling Act 2005 (Prize Gaming) (Permits) Regulations 2007. The fees payable are £300 for a new permit and the same sum for the renewal after ten years.

CASINOS

Types of casino

The Act imposes a limit of one regional, eight large and eight small casinos. The Government have announced that there will not be a regional casino but the eight large and eight small casinos will be allowed.

Regional Casino	Minimum area exclusively for casino table games	1,000 sq metres
	Minimum additional gambling area	2,500 sq metres
	Minimum non-gambling area	1,500 sq metres
Large Casino	Minimum area exclusively for casino table games	1,000 sq metres
	Minimum additional gambling area	Nil
	Minimum non-gambling area	500 sq metres
Small Casino	Minimum area exclusively for casino table games	500 sq metres
	Minimum additional gambling area	Nil
	Minimum non-gambling area	250 sq metres

Limits on numbers of machines, stakes and prizes

Category A machines – Regional casino only

Unlimited stakes and unlimited prizes.

The maximum number of machines irrespective of number of gaming tables is limited to 1,250.

The legislation provides that there must be one table available for play in respect of every 25 gaming machines. Therefore, for a regional casino to provide 1,250 machines there must be a minimum of 50 gaming tables available for play.

Category B1 to D machines – All casinos

A large casino is permitted five gaming machines for each gaming table available for play, up to a maximum of 150 machines.

A small casino is permitted to have up to 80 machines but it is necessary to have one gaming table available for play every two gaming machines.

The stake and prize limits are as follows:

Category B1   Maximum stake £2. Maximum prize £4,000.

Category B2   Maximum stake £100 per game; £15 per chip. Maximum prize £500.

Category B3   Maximum stake £1. Maximum prize £500.

Category B4   Maximum stake £1. Maximum prize £250.

Category C   Maximum stake 50p. Maximum prize £35.

Category D   Maximum stake 10p (30p when non-exchangeable prizes). Maximum prize £5 cash or £8 non-cash.

Advertising

A code of practice was issued in August 2007 regarding advertising by casinos.

Any advertising by casino operators must comply with the Code which requires that:

(a) advertisements should comply with the Committee of Advertising Practice (CAP) and Broadcast Committee of Advertising Practice (BCAP) rules;

(b) advertisements must be legal and not misleading;

(c) advertisements and promotions should be socially responsible as described in the CAP and BCAP Rules;

(d) care must be taken not to exploit children and other vulnerable persons in relation to gambling activity; and

(e)   advertisements should not be specifically and intentionally targeted towards people under the age of 18 through the selection of media, style of presentation, content or context in which they appear. All advertisers and gambling operators should already be aware that it is an offence under section 46 of the Gambling Act 2005 to invite a child or young person to gamble.

Any advertising by a casino has to include the website address www.gambleaware.co.uk.

The Code requires that no gambling products (with the exception of bingo) may be advertised on television before the accepted watershed time of 9.00pm.

Other gambling products
Regional casinos and large casinos are able to provide betting and bingo. Small casinos are only able to provide bingo.

Casino operating licences
Consideration of applications: general principles
Section 70 sets out the general principles which the Commission applies in determining applications, and particular matters which they may take into account. The two main matters are the licensing objectives and the applicant's suitability. Integrity, competence and financial circumstances are among the factors that can be taken into account. The assessment may also cover the suitability of equipment to be used in connection with the proposed activities.

Subsection (3) makes specific provisions for those cases where the application is for a non-remote casino operating licence. In such cases, the Commission must have regard to the applicant's commitment to protecting vulnerable people from being harmed or exploited by gambling, and to making assistance available to people who may be affected by problem gambling.

Consideration of application: criminal record

One of the licensing objectives is to prevent gambling being associated with, or being a source of, crime or disorder. The Commission may refuse an application for an operating licence if the applicant has a conviction for a relevant offence. This is without prejudice to the suitability of the applicant generally. (Section 71.)

Consideration of application: demand

Section 72 removes the principle that whether or not there is demand for a new casino is a factor to be taken into account when applications are considered. It also abolishes the previous statutory provisions regarding "permitted areas for casinos".

The process for issuing new casino premises licences

If a Licensing Authority is selected as one of the areas where a new casino will be located, the authority will have to invite applications for the licences. How this process will be carried out will be set out in regulations. If more applications are received than the number of available licences, the Licensing Authority must determine whether each application would be granted if there was no limit on the number of licences the authority could grant. Each application will have to be considered separately and no reference made to the other applications received. Each of the other applicants will be considered "interested parties" and may make representations. At the end of the first stage, the result will be one or more provisional decisions to grant a premises licence. As with any other decision with the Licensing Authority, this provisional decision may be appealed against. If an appeal is lodged, the Licensing Authority cannot move to the second stage until any appeals have been determined.

The second stage only applies where the number of applications that the Licensing Authority would provisionally grant as a result of the stage one process exceeds the number of available casino premises licences.

Under the second stage, the Licensing Authority has to decide between the competing applicants and grant any available licences to those applications that in their opinion will result in the greatest benefit to their areas. The principles which the Licensing Authority are going to apply in determining the stage two competition must be set out in the Licensing Authority's policy.

There is no right of appeal against the grant or refusal at stage two other than by way of judicial review.

BETTING

Betting premises

The legislation contains one licence for betting premises.

Whilst there is only one betting premises licence, there are two operating licences that can be issued in respect of betting. A general betting (limited) operating licence is one that means:

(a)   a non-remote general betting operating licence which is subject to a condition that the licensee may not hold a betting premises licence; or

(b)   a remote general betting operating licence that is issued subject to conditions that the licensee cannot hold a non-remote betting operating licence, that they may only provide facilities for betting by telephone and that the annual gross yield does not exceed £250,000.

A general betting (standard) operating licence is:

(a)   a non-remote general betting operating licence that is not a limited operating licence; or

(b)   a remote general betting operating licence that is not a limited operating licence.

The betting premises licence covers betting shops and also track betting, i.e. betting at racecourses, dog tracks and other places where sporting events are held.

Persons below the age of 18 cannot enter a betting shop. However, in respect of betting at tracks, under-18s can enter the area where betting is taking place on days when races are being held.

Under section 181, the Licensing Authority may attach conditions restricting the number of betting machines installed in betting shops, the type of machines and the circumstances under which the machines are made available. This power only relates to betting machines which are different to fixed-odds betting terminals. When considering applications for betting premises licences, the size of the premises, where machines are situated in the premises and whether the staff are able to monitor their use by anyone under the age of 18 or by a vulnerable person and also the number of positions where people can place bets, are among the factors the Authority can take into account.

Track betting

Tracks are sites, including horse racecourses and dog tracks, where races or other sporting events take place, e.g. football grounds and cricket grounds.

Premises licence

An applicant for a betting premises licence for betting at tracks does not need to hold an operating licence. However, there will be a mandatory condition attached to any premises licence for betting at tracks, that the holder of the premises licence must ensure that everyone who takes bets does have a relevant operating licence.

Occasional use notices

Betting on a track is permitted by an occasional use notice for up to eight days in a calendar year, i.e. 1 January to 31 December.

The notice for occasional use must be served on the Licensing Authority and the police. Notices can be given for a continuous period of eight days (section 39).

Gaming machines on tracks

A betting premises licence in respect of a track does not give an automatic entitlement to use gaming machines. However, if the track operator holding the premises licence also holds a pool betting operating licence then up to four gaming machines of Category B2 to D can be used.

Pool betting

Pool betting may be offered at a horse racecourse by the tote and at a dog track by the holder of a premises licence for the track (section 180).

Self-contained betting offices on tracks

There can be self-contained betting offices on tracks. These must be very clearly indicated as no-one under 18 can go into that part of the premises.

On course betting

Section 151 of the Act requires applicants for premises licences to submit plans of the premises. Licensing Authorities should, in their policies, set out the information they will require which should include the detailed plans for the racecourse itself and the area that will be used for temporary "on course betting".

REMOTE GAMBLING

Section 4 of the Gambling Act 2005 defines remote gambling as gambling in which people participate by the use of remote communication.

"Remote communication" means communication using:

(a)   the internet;

(b)   the telephone;

(c)   the television;

(d)   the radio; or

(e)   any other kind of electronic or other technology for facilitating communication.

Section 67 enables the Gambling Commission to issue a remote operating licence to enable remote gambling to be carried on. Section 89 of the Act sets out the principles the Gambling Commission will apply when deciding whether or not to grant a remote operating licence.

Subsections 3 to 6 of section 89 enable the Commission to set standards relating to the consideration of applications for remote operating licences. The Commission can enforce these standards through licence conditions, including the testing of the operator's systems.

It is a requirement of a remote operating licence that remote gambling equipment used by the operator in providing facilities for gambling must be located in Great Britain. This is set out in section 89(1).

Section 89(2) empowers the Commission to depart from this general requirement, in certain circumstances. The Commission may allow an operator to site particular pieces of specified remote gambling equipment off-shore, provided the Commission is satisfied that to do so is consistent with the licensing objectives in section 1.

The Commission has the discretion to establish standards in respect of remote gambling. If such standards are established, they will be taken into account when dealing with applications for remote operating licences.

LOTTERIES

The Gambling Commission can issue lottery operating licences to:

(a)   non-commercial societies;

(b)   local authorities and external lottery managers (section 98(1)).

A non-commercial society is a society established for cultural or sporting purposes or for a purpose that is something other than private gain.

A lottery is unlawful unless there is an operating licence issued by the Gambling Commission or it is an exempt lottery. The exemptions are:

(a)   incidental non-commercial lotteries, e.g. the raffle or tombola at the Christmas fayre;

(b)   private lotteries, e.g. work or residence lotteries;

(c)   customer lotteries, e.g. a lottery run by someone running a business in this country. Tickets can only be available when the person receiving the ticket is on the business premises as a customer, only the business can provide tickets and the lottery cannot be advertised anywhere else;

(d)   small society lotteries which are registered by a local authority.

Small lotteries

As long as the proceeds from one lottery do not exceed £20,000 or the total income from all the lotteries run by an organisation do not exceed £250,000 in a calendar year, the lottery is classed as a small lottery. If an organisation prints

25,000 tickets for sale at £1 each, this is automatically a large lottery as the total income from that one lottery could exceed £20,000. Provided the lottery does not exceed the two thresholds of £20,000 or £250,000, lotteries can lawfully be run by being registered with the local authority as a small lottery.

Lottery operating licence

Section 99 provides that six mandatory conditions must be attached to lottery operating licences:

1.   20% of the proceeds must be applied to the purposes of the promoting society.

2.   The proceeds of any lottery may not exceed £2,000,000 and the total proceeds of all lotteries promoted in a calendar year cannot exceed £10,000,000.

3.   The maximum prize may not exceed £25,000 or, if more than this amount, 10% of the proceeds of the lottery. If there is a rollover, it must comply with this provision.

4.   Tickets must identify the promoting society, who is responsible for the promotion of the lottery and give the date of the draw.

5.   The prices of all tickets must be the same and must be shown on the tickets.

6.   Membership of the group of people among whom prizes in any lottery are allocated may not be dependent on making any payment apart from purchasing a ticket.

Promoting a lottery

Under section 252(1), a person promotes a lottery if he/she makes or participates in making the arrangements for a lottery.

A person promotes a lottery if he/she:

(a) makes arrangements for the printing of lottery tickets;

(b) makes arrangements for the printing of promotional material;

(c) arranges for the distribution or publication of promotional material;

(d) possesses promotional material with a view to its distribution or publication,

(e) makes other arrangements to advertise a lottery;

(f) invites a person to participate in a lottery;

(g) sells or supplies a lottery ticket;

(h) offers to sell or supply a lottery ticket;

(i) possesses a lottery ticket with a view to its sale or supply;

(j) does or offers to do anything by virtue of which a person becomes a member of a class among whom prizes in a lottery are to be allocated; or

(k) uses premises for the purpose of allocating prizes or for any other purpose connected with the administration of a lottery (section 252(2)).

"Promotional material" means a document which:

(a) advertises a specified lottery;

(b) invites participation in a specified lottery;

(c) contains information about how to participate in a specified lottery; or

(d) lists winners in a specified lottery (section 252(3)).

Offences

Promotion of a lottery

Section 258 makes it an offence to promote a lottery. However, as long as the person promoting the lottery holds the relevant operating licence or acts on behalf of a person who has been granted such a licence, no offence is committed.

If the lottery is an exempt lottery (see below) then no offence is committed. The following lotteries are exempt:

(a)   incidental non-commercial lotteries;

(b)   private lotteries;

(c)   customer lotteries;

(d)   small society lotteries registered with the Licensing Authority.

Facilitating a lottery

If a person prints tickets for a lottery, prints promotional material for a lottery or advertises one, an offence is committed unless there is a relevant operating licence in force or the lottery is an exempt lottery (section 259).

Misusing profits of lottery

Section 260 provides for a general offence of misusing the profits of a lottery, e.g. using the proceeds for a purpose other than that specified on the tickets.

Misusing profits of an exempt lottery

It is an offence for someone to use the proceeds of an exempt lottery for the purpose other than the one for which the lottery was permitted to be promoted (section 261).

Exempt lotteries

Schedule 11 sets out the various categories of exempt lotteries and the principles that apply to them.

Incidental non-commercial lotteries (Part 1)

Incidental non-commercial lotteries are activities such as the raffle and tombola at a garden party. The lottery must be a small part of a wider ranging fund-raising event, the proceeds of which are not for any private gain.

To be a non-commercial lottery:

(a) the promoters may only deduct such sums for prizes and other costs as are prescribed in regulations;

(b) the lottery must be promoted purely for a non-commercial purpose, i.e. there must be no element of private gain;

(c) there cannot be a rollover; and

(d) tickets must only be available at the event while it is taking place and the results announced at the event.

Private lotteries (Part 2)

There are three types of "private lottery" which qualify as exempt lotteries:

1. A private society lottery is a lottery promoted by members of a society who have been authorised to run it and people who purchase tickets are members of that organisation or are on the premises wholly or mainly used for society purposes.

2. A works lottery is a lottery if the promoters work in a single set of premises and everyone who purchases the tickets also works in the same premises.

3. A residents' lottery is a lottery where the promoters live in a single set of premises and tickets can only be purchased by people living in the same premises.

Private lotteries cannot advertise apart from on the relevant premises, e.g. a works lottery can only advertise on the premises where the people entitled to purchase the tickets work. In addition, tickets will have to give the name and address of the promoter, specify who can buy tickets and explain that the rights in tickets cannot be transferred.

Every ticket must be sold for the same price, which must be shown on the tickets and the tickets have to be paid for before a prize can be allocated.

Customer lottery (Part 3)

Anyone running a business and occupying business premises in Great Britain can run a customer lottery. Tickets can only be obtained by people when they are on the business's premises as a customer of the business. The lottery can only be advertised on those premises. Tickets can only be obtained from the business promoting the lottery.

The tickets must give the name and address of the promoter, specify who is entitled to purchase the tickets and explain that the rights under the ticket cannot be transferred. The price for the tickets has to be the same and must be shown on the tickets. No profit can be made for running a customer lottery. There can only be one draw a week and the maximum prize is £50. However, there is no limit to the number of prizes that may be given each week.

The customer lottery may be run by any business. Some public houses have a 'lucky number' draw – the winning number being the bonus ball for the National Lottery. As long as the prize does not exceed £50 this can be lawfully operated as a customer lottery.

Small society lotteries (Parts 4 and 5)

A non-commercial society that runs a lottery where the income is below certain specified thresholds can register with the local authority.

Financial limits are that the proceeds for one individual lottery cannot exceed £20,000 and in a calendar year the total proceeds do not exceed £250,000 (Sch 11, para 31(2) and (3)).

The organisation must produce tickets identifying the name of the society, the price of the ticket, the name of the promoter and the date of the draw (Sch 11, para 36). The price of the tickets must be the same (Sch 11, para 37).

The organisation must be registered with the local authority. The form of application is prescribed by Regulation 3 of the Small Society Lotteries (Registration of Non-Commercial Societies) Regulations 2007.

As soon as practicable after receiving an application, the local authority must register the society, tell the applicant that this has been done and notify the Gambling Commission (Sch 11, para 44).

The local authority must refuse an application for registration if, within five years ending with the date of the application, the applicant has had an operating licence revoked by the Gambling Commission or an application for one refused (Sch 11, para 47).

In addition, the local authority may refuse to register an applicant if they think:

(a) the applicant is not a non-commercial society;

(b) someone who will or may be connected with the promotion of the lottery has been convicted of a relevant offence; or

(c) false or misleading information has been provided in connection with the application (Sch 11, para 48).

If the local authority does register a lottery and later finds that they would have had grounds for refusing the application, the registration can be revoked (Sch 11, para 50).

Registration may not be revoked without giving the society an opportunity to make representations (Sch 11, para 50(3)). If it is decided to revoke the registration, revocation can take place immediately or at some date in the future but no longer than two months after the decision (Sch 11, para 50).

This provision would enable a Licensing Authority to delay the revocation of a registration in circumstances where the organisation involved was currently running a lottery and the draw was due to take place in the near future. The Licensing Authority may take the view that it would be very difficult for the money people had paid to purchase tickets to be returned, so the better option would be to let the draw take place and then cancel the registration.

If the local authority refuses to register a society or cancels a registration, there is a right of appeal to the magistrates' court (Sch 11, para 51).

The society must pay the annual fee to the local authority or the registration can be cancelled (Sch 11, para 54). The fee for initial registration is £40 and the annnual fee is £20.

CHAIN-GIFT SCHEMES

For a long time there has been concern about pyramid selling, otherwise known as chain-gift schemes. These schemes rely on an individual paying to take part and their financial gain depends on how many other people they can persuade to join in.

Under section 43(1), anyone who invites another person to join in a chain-gift scheme or knowingly participates in the promotion, administration or management of such a scheme commits an offence.

OPERATING LICENCE CONDITIONS

The Gambling Commission can attach conditions to operating licences and, in addition, codes of practice have been issued which operators are expected to comply with. Among the mandatory conditions are the following:

1. **All operating licences except gaming machine technical, gambling software, bingo and casino ancillary remote licences, and lottery licences issued to non-commercial societies or local authorities.**

   Licensees who hold customer funds for use in future gambling must set out clearly, in information made available to customers in writing, whether they protect customers' funds in the event of insolvency, and the method by which this is achieved.

2. **All operating licences except for gaming machine technical, gambling software and remote operating licences.**

   Licensees, as part of their internal controls and financial accounting systems, must have in place and follow written policies and procedures concerning the handling of cash and cash equivalents (i.e. banker's drafts, cheques and debit cards), designed to minimise the risk of crimes such as money laundering, to avoid the giving of illicit credit and to provide assurance that gambling activities are being conducted fairly.

3. **Gaming machine general operating licences for adult gaming centres and family entertainment centres.**

   Licensees must not:

   (a) themselves provide credit in connection with gambling; and

   (b) participate in, arrange, permit or knowingly facilitate the giving of credit in connection with gambling.

CODES OF PRACTICE

Remote and non-remote casino licensees
Ordinary Code provision

As part of their procedures for compliance with the requirements of the Proceeds of Crime Act 2002, the 2003 Money Laundering Regulations and the Terrorism Act 2000, licensees should have procedures in place which:

(a)　establish procedures of internal control and communication to prevent money laundering;

(b)　establish, verify and record the identity of all customers who enter the gambling facilities;

(c)　record all transactions above those levels set out in Gambling Commission guidance;

(d)　keep those records in a form and for the period required by the 2003 Money Laundering Regulations;

(e)　ensure that, as required by law, reports of any apparent suspicious activity are passed in a timely manner to the Money Laundering Reporting Officer, whose job it is to consider such reports and to forward them where appropriate to the Serious Organised Crime Agency; and

(f)　provide appropriate training to relevant staff to make them aware of the requirements of the laws on money laundering in respect of the operator's business and to enable them to recognise and deal with transactions which may be related to money laundering.

All licensees
Social Responsibility Code provision

Licensees must have and put into effect policies and procedures intended to promote socially responsible gambling.

Licensees' policies and procedures for socially responsible gambling must include but need not be confined to:

(a)   the specific policies and procedures required to secure compliance with the Code;

(b)   a commitment to, and how they will contribute to research into, the prevention and treatment of problem gambling;

(c)   a commitment to, and how they will contribute to, public education on the risks of gambling and how to gamble safely; and

(d)   a commitment to, and how they will contribute to, the identification of and treatment of problem gamblers.

Non-remote casino licensees (except a regional casino) and adult gaming centres

Social Responsibility Code provision

Licensees must have and put into effect policies and procedures designed to prevent underage gambling, and monitor the effectiveness of these.

Such procedures must include:

(a)   checking the age of apparently underage customers;

(b)   removing anyone who appears to be underage who tries to access the gambling facilities and cannot produce an acceptable form of identification; and

(c)   taking action when there are attempts by under-18s to enter the premises.

Licensees must not deliberately provide facilities for gambling in such a way as to appeal particularly to children or young people, for example by reflecting or being associated with youth culture.

In premises restricted to adults, service should be refused in any circumstances where any adult is accompanied by a child or young person.

Licensees must take all reasonable steps to ensure that all staff understand their responsibilities for preventing underage gambling. This should include appropriate training which must cover the legal requirements on returning stakes and not paying prizes to underage customers.

Licensees must only accept identification which:

(a) contains a photograph from which the individual can be identified;

(b) states the individual's date of birth;

(c) is valid; and

(d) is legible and has no visible signs of tampering or reproduction.

Non-remote general betting licensees and non-remote betting intermediaries

Social Responsibility Code provision

Licensees must have and put into effect policies and procedures designed to prevent underage gambling, and monitor the effectiveness of these.

Such procedures must include:

(a) checking the age of apparently underage customers;

(b) removing from adult-only licensed premises anyone who appears to be underage who tries to access the gambling facilities and cannot produce an acceptable form of identification;

(c) taking action when there are attempts by under-18s to enter adult-only premises;

(d)   refusing entry to any adult-only area of a track to anyone unable to produce an acceptable form of identification; and

(e)   taking action when there are unlawful attempts to enter the adult-only areas.

Licensees must not deliberately provide facilities for gambling in such a way as to appeal particularly to children or young people, for example by reflecting or being associated with youth culture.

In premises restricted to adults, service should be refused in any circumstances where any adult is accompanied by a child or young person.

Licensees must take all reasonable steps to ensure that all staff understand their responsibilities for preventing underage gambling. This should include appropriate training which must cover the legal requirements on returning stakes and not paying prizes to underage customers.

Licensees must only accept identification which:

(a)   contains a photograph from which the individual can be identified;

(b)   states the individual's date of birth;

(c)   is valid; and

(d)   is legible and has no visible signs of tampering or reproduction.

Remote licensees (including ancillary remote betting licensees) but not gaming machine technical, gambling software, ancillary remote casino or ancillary remote bingo licensees

Social Responsibility Code provision

Licensees must have and put into effect policies and procedures designed to prevent underage gambling, and monitor the effectiveness of these.

Such procedures must include:

(a) warning potential customers that underage gambling is an offence;

(b) requiring customers to affirm that they are of legal age;

(c) regularly reviewing their age verification systems and implementing all reasonable improvements that may be made as technology advances and as information improves;

(d) ensuring that relevant staff are properly trained in the use of their age verification procedures. In particular, customer services staff must be appropriately trained in the use of secondary forms of identification when initial verification procedures fail to prove that an individual is of legal age;

(e) enabling their gambling websites to permit filtering software to be used by adults (such as parents or within schools) in order to restrict access to relevant pages of those sites;

(f) in the case of any UK resident customer who registers to gamble and deposits money using a debit card or any other type of electronic payment method other than a credit card, unless the licensee has established that a third party has satisfactorily carried out age verification, such procedures should also include:

    (i) verifying additional information about the customer, such as carrying out credit checks and searching databases which list names and addresses of individuals over the age of 18;

    (ii) carrying out secondary age verification checks in any circumstances which give the operator reason to suspect that the person may be underage;

(iii) not permitting the customer to withdraw any winnings from their account until age verification has been satisfactorily completed; and

(iv) in any event, a requirement that if age verification has not been satisfactorily completed within 72 hours of the customer applying to register to gamble and depositing money:

- the account will be frozen;

- no further gambling will be permitted until age verification has been successfully completed; and

- if on completion of age verification the customer is shown to be underage, all stakes will be returned to the customer and no winnings paid;

(g) in the case of any non-UK resident customer who registers to gamble and deposits money using a debit card or any other type of electronic payment method other than a credit card, such procedures should also include:

(i) taking all reasonable steps to make use of information publicly available for age verification purposes from whichever country the potential customer is resident in; and

(ii) each of the steps outlined in (f) above, unless the licensee can demonstrate to the Commission's satisfaction that that step could not reasonably be implemented, or in the case of requirement (iv) above, that a period of more than 72 hours was reasonably required;

(h) in the case of any customer who registers to gamble and deposits money using a credit card, conducting a programme of random checks of credit card users for compliance with age restrictions.

All licensees except gaming machine technical and gambling software and bingo and casino ancillary remote licensees

Social Responsibility Code provision

Licensees must make information readily available to their customers on how to gamble responsibly and how to access information about, and help in respect of, problem gambling.

Licensees must take all reasonable steps to ensure that this information is readily accessible, including in locations which enable the customer to obtain it discreetly.

For gambling premises this should include:

(a) information in the gambling area, near gaming machines and near to where ATMs are located;

(b) posters, or leaflets that may be collected discreetly and taken away, in other areas (e.g. toilets and near to exit doors).

The information must be prominent, and appropriate to the size and layout of the premises.

The information must cover where relevant:

(a) the availability of measures that are accessible to help an individual monitor or control their gambling, such as to restrict the duration of a gambling session or the amount of money they can spend;

(b)   the availability of timers or any other forms of reminders or "reality checks" that may be available;

(c)   self-exclusion options; and

(d)   information about the availability of further help or advice.

The information must be directed to all customers who wish to enjoy gambling as entertainment and not be targeted only at those the operator perceives to be "problem gamblers".

Non-remote casino, bingo and general betting licensees, adult gaming centres, and remote licensees other than gaming machine technical, gambling software, remote lotteries, and ancillary remote bingo and casino licensees

Social Responsibility Code provision

Licensees must implement policies and procedures for customer interaction where they have concerns that a customer's behaviour may indicate problem gambling. The policies must include:

1.   Identification of the appropriate level of management who may initiate customer interaction and the procedures for doing so.

2.   The types of behaviour that will be logged/reported to the appropriate level of staff and which may trigger customer interaction at an appropriate moment.

3.   The circumstances in which consideration should be given to refusing service to customers and/or barring them from the operator's gambling premises.

4.   Training for all staff on their respective responsibilities, in particular so that they know who is designated to deal with problem gambling issues.

Such policies and procedures should be consistent with, and implemented with due regard to, licensees' duties in respect of the health and safety of their staff.

Non-remote casino, bingo, betting and lottery licensees, and adult gaming centres

Social Responsibility Code provision

Licensees must put in place procedures for self-exclusion and take all reasonable steps to refuse service or to otherwise prevent an individual who has entered a self-exclusion agreement from participating in gambling.

Licensees must take steps to remove the name and details of a self-excluded individual from any marketing databases used by the company or group (or otherwise flag that person as an individual to whom marketing material must not be sent), within two days of receiving the completed self-exclusion notification.

Licensees must take all reasonable steps to prevent any marketing material being sent to a self-excluded customer as soon as practicable.

This covers any marketing material relating to gambling, or other activities that take place on the premises where gambling may take place. However, it would not extend to blanket marketing which is targeted at a particular geographical area and where the excluded individual would not knowingly be included.

Licensees must close any customer accounts of an individual who has entered a self-exclusion agreement and return any funds held in the customer account. It is not sufficient merely to prevent an individual from withdrawing funds from their customer account whilst still accepting wagers from them. Where the giving of credit is permitted, the licensee may retain details of the amount owed to them by the individual, although the account must not be active.

Licensees must implement procedures designed to ensure that an individual who has self-excluded cannot gain access to gambling; and which include:

1.   A register of those excluded with appropriate records (name, address, other details, and any membership or account details that may be held by the operator).

2.   Photo identification (where available and in particular where enforcement of the system may depend on photographic ID), and a signature.

3.   Staff training to ensure that staff are able to enforce the systems.

4.   The removal of those persons found in the gambling area or attempting to gamble from the premises.

Adult gaming centre licensees/family entertainment centre licensees

Ordinary Code provision

Licensees who employ children (under-16s) and young persons (those aged 16 and 17) should be aware that it is an offence:

(a)   to employ them to provide facilities for gambling;

(b)   if gaming machines are sited on the premises, for their contracts of employment to require them, or for them to be permitted, to perform a function in connection with a gaming machine at any time; and

(c)   to employ them to carry out any other function on adult gaming centre licensed premises while any gambling activity is being carried on in reliance on the premises licence (adult gaming centres only).

As to (b), it should be noted that in the Commission's view

the relevant provision of the Act applies to any function performed in connection with a gaming machine. This includes servicing or cleaning such a machine.

Accordingly, licensees should have policies and procedures designed to ensure that:

(a)   children and young persons are never asked to perform tasks within (a) or (b) above;

(b)   all staff, including those who are children or young persons themselves, are instructed about the laws relating to access to gambling by children and young persons;

and should consider adopting a policy that:

(a)   children and young persons are not employed to work on adult gaming centre licensed premises at any time when the premises are open for business; and

(b)   gaming machines are turned off if children and young persons are working on the premises outside the hours when the premises are open for business.

Part 3
PREMISES LICENCES

THE LICENSING AUTHORITY

Licensing Authorities are responsible for issuing premises licences. The following local authorities are Licensing Authorities for the purposes of the Gambling Act 2005: district councils; county councils for counties where there are no district councils; London borough councils; the Common Council of the City of London; the Council of the Isles of Scilly; and, in relation to Wales, county councils and county borough councils.

The Committee of any such council already established under the Licensing Act 2003 is responsible for dealing with applications for premises licences under the Gambling Act 2005.

All the powers under the Gambling Act 2005 are delegated to this Licensing Committee, with the exceptions of:

(a)   functions relating to resolutions by the Licensing Authority not to issue casino premises licenses;

(b)   formulation of the three-year licensing policy; and

(c)   determination of premises licence fees.

The first two matters are not and cannot be delegated to a Licensing Committee but must be taken by the full council. Decisions on fees are not automatically delegated but may be. If the authority decides to delegate the responsibility for determining fees, the power can be delegated to the Licensing Committee, sub-committee or an officer.

Policy
For each three-year period, the Licensing Authority have to prepare a statement of the principles that they propose to apply in exercising their functions under the Act and publish that statement. They must review that statement from time to time and, if necessary, review it. Under section 154(2)(c), the policy must be made by the full council.

Under section 349 of the Gambling Act 2005, in preparing the statement or a revision, the Licensing Authority must consult:

(a)   the police;

(b)   the fire authority;

(c)   one or more persons who appear to the Authority to represent the interests of persons carrying on gambling businesses in the Authority's area; and

(d)   one or more or persons who appear to the Authority to represent the interests of persons who are likely to be affected by the exercise of the Authority's functions under the Act.

The Secretary of State appointed 31 January 2007 as the day the first policy was to come into force (Article 2, Gambling Act 2005 (Licensing Authority Policy Statement) (First Appointed Day) Order 2006). In addition, the Secretary of State has made regulations about:

(a)   the form the statement will take;

(b)   the procedure to be followed in relation to the preparation, review or revision of the statement;

(c)   the publication of statements.

The policy will last until 30 January 2010. Before this date the Licensing Authority will have to have reviewed the policy. The review procedure will include consulting the people referred to in section 349 of the Gambling Act 2005. Any revision of the policy must be published at least four weeks before it comes into force. The revised policy must be available on the Authority's website and in public libraries or other premises in the Licensing Authority's area. In addition, the fact of the publication of the policy must be advertised on the Authority's website and in one or more of the following ways:

1. In a local newspaper circulating in the Authority's area.

2. In a local newsletter, circular or similar document circulating in the area of the Authority.

3. On a public notice board in or near the principal office of the Authority.

4. On a public notice board on the premises of public libraries in the Authority's area (Regulation 7, Gambling Act 2005 (Licensing Authority Policy Statement) (England and Wales) Regulations 2006).

Contents of the policy

Regulation 4 of the Gambling Act 2005 (Licensing Authority Policy Statement) (England and Wales) Regulations 2006 provides that the policy should contain a number of matters:

1. A summary of the matters contained in the policy, including the geographical area of the Authority and who was consulted on the policy.

2. Principles to be applied by the Authority when designating in writing a body which is competent to advise about the protection of children from harm. This will normally, but need not necessarily, be the Local Safeguarding Children Body.

3. Principles to be applied in deciding whether a person is an "interested party", e.g. the size of the premises, the nature of the activities to be carried out.

4. A statement of the principles to be applied regarding inspection/enforcement, e.g. the regulatory compliance code (the Enforcement Concordat).

5. Factors the Authority may consider when dealing with applications for premises licences/permits and

when deciding whether or not to review a premises licence, e.g. proximity to schools, vulnerable adults centres, residential areas with a high concentration of children.

6.   If the Authority passes a resolution regarding "no casinos", this must be included in the policy.

7.   Details of how information will be exchanged with the police/Gambling Commission.

8.   If the Authority sets out the principles to be applied when considering family entertainment centre permits, this can be included in the policy.

9.   In respect of casinos, there is a two-stage application process and the policy must set out the principles the Authority are going to apply to the application when considering the second stage.

10.   In respect of prize gaming permits, the policy must set out the principles the Authority intend to apply when considering applications for permits. In particular, any matter that they may take into account when considering the suitability of applicants should be set out.

The Authority should also set out how they intend to approach the licensing objectives.

Preventing gambling from being a source of crime or disorder, being associated with crime or disorder or being used to support crime

The Gambling Commission will play a leading role in preventing gambling from being a source of crime. However, the Licensing Authority would need to consider the location of premises in the context of this licensing objective, e.g. residential areas, and can also consider the steps that may be necessary to prevent disorder, e.g. door supervisors.

Ensuring gambling is conducted in a fair and open way

It is not expected that Licensing Authorities will become concerned with ensuring that gambling is conducted in a fair and open way as this will either be for the management of the gambling business, and therefore subject to the operating licence, or will be in relation to the suitability and actions of the individual. However, in relation to the licensing of tracks for betting, the Authority's role will be different from other premises in that track operators will not necessarily have an operating licence. In those circumstances, the premises licence may need to contain conditions to ensure that the environment in which the betting takes place is suitable. Information on the likely conditions and the approach to track betting licences should be set out in the policy.

Protecting children and other vulnerable persons from being harmed or exploited by gambling

Licensing Authorities will need to consider whether specific measures will be required to protect children on particular categories of premises where they may be admitted. This may include requirements such as the supervision of entrances, segregation of gambling from areas frequented by children and supervision of gaming machines in non-adult gambling specific premises.

As far as "vulnerable persons" are concerned, this would include people who gamble more than they want to, people who gamble beyond their means, and people who may not be able to make informed or balanced decisions about gambling due to a mental impairment, alcohol or drugs.

Licensing Authorities will need to consider, in relation to particular premises, whether any special considerations should apply in relation to the protection of vulnerable persons. These should be mentioned in the policy.

Functions

When carrying out their functions under the Act, the Licensing Authority shall aim to permit the use of premises for gambling, so far as the Authority think it is:

(a)   in accordance with any relevant code of practice;

(b)   in accordance with any relevant guidance issued by the Gambling Commission;

(c)   reasonably consistent with the licensing objectives; and

(d)   in accordance with the Licensing Authority policy (section 153(1)).

Demand is not a relevant factor to take into account when dealing with applications for premises licences (section 153(2)).

If representations are made to an application, the matter must be referred to the members of the Licensing Committee unless the representations are withdrawn (section 162(1)).

Register

The Authority must maintain a register of all premises licences issued by the Authority and the register must be available for inspection by members of the public. The Secretary of State can make regulations regarding the form of the register and the manner in which it is maintained (section 156). No regulations had been made regarding the form of the register at the time of publication of this book.

Planning permission

Section 210 makes it clear that a Licensing Authority is not to have regard to Planning or Building Regulations matters when considering an application for a premises licence. It also provides that any decision on the application by a

Licensing Authority is not to constrain a later decision by the Authority under Planning or Building Regulations.

APPLICATIONS FOR PREMISES LICENCES

An application for a premises licence is made to the Licensing Authority within whose area the premises are wholly or partly situated. An application can only be made by a person who holds an operating licence authorising them to carry on the activity in respect of which the premises licence is sought, or who has applied for an operating licence. In addition, the application can only be made by a person who has a right to occupy the premises to which the application relates. Even though a person has not yet been granted an operating licence, if an application has been made to the Gambling Commission for an operating licence which authorises the applicant to carry on the activity in respect of which the premises licence is sought, an application can be submitted for a premises licence. If this situation does arise, the Licensing Authority cannot determine the application for the premises licence until the operating licence has been issued (section 163(2)).

The "right to occupy" the premises must be a lease or a freehold interest in the premises. A lease containing a condition that if the premises licence was not granted the lease would be void is a sufficient legal right to occupy the premises.

The application must be made in the prescribed form, contain or be accompanied by the prescribed information or documents and accompanied by the fee.

The Gambling Act 2005 (Premises Licences and Provisional Statements) Regulations 2007 set out the procedure to be followed by applicants for premises licences and prescribe forms to be used by applicants as well as the forms to be used by Licensing Authorities to notify people of their decision. The Gambling (Premises Licence Fees) (England and Wales) Regulations 2007 set out the fees to be paid.

The application form prescribed by the Regulations requires applicants to state the activities they wish to carry out on the premises, details of the premises and the hours of the proposed activities. There are no specific sections where the applicant has to set out the steps they intend to take to meet the licensing objectives. However, in the application form for an operating licence, applicants do have to set out how they will meet the three licensing objectives.

The application form has to be served on the Licensing Authority. The applicant will also have to serve all the responsible authorities with a notice prescribed by Schedule 6 to the 2007 Regulations.

A plan will have to be submitted with the application form. The plan must be to scale but the Regulations do not prescribe a specific scale: the applicant will be able to determine this. The plan must show the boundary of the premises, the entrances and exits, the location of toilets and the areas where gambling will be carried out. In respect of applications for bingo premises licences or family entertainment centre premises licences, the plan must show the nature and location of any barrier or other thing separating any part of the premises in which (in bingo halls) Category B or C machines are located and (in respect of family entertainment centres) where Category C machines are situated.

As far as public notice is concerned, the Regulations require a notice to be displayed on or near the premises where it can conveniently be read by members of the public from the exterior of the premises. This notice must be maintained for 28 days from the day on which the application is made to the Licensing Authority. In addition, a notice must be inserted in a local newspaper or, if there is none, a local newsletter, circular or similar document circulating in the Authority's area, within ten days of the application being made.

Under Regulation 14, if an applicant fails to publish proper notice of their application within the period specified in the Regulations, either by not displaying the notice for 28 days, putting the notice in a position where it cannot be easily read by the public or failing to publish notice in the local press, the Authority cannot determine the application. The applicant should properly advertise their application and, from the time the proper advertising takes place, interested parties and responsible authorities have 28 days to make representations to the Licensing Authority.

Responsible authorities/interested parties (sections 157/158)

It is only responsible authorities and interested parties who can make representations to an application.

Responsible authorities are:

(a)   a Licensing Authority in whose area the premises are wholly or partly situated;

(b)   the Gambling Commission;

(c)   the police;

(d)   the fire authority;

(e)   the local planning authority in accordance with the Town and Country Planning Act for an area in which the premises are wholly or partly situated;

(f)   an authority which has functions by virtue of an enactment in respect of minimising or preventing the risk of pollution of the environment or of harm to human health in an area in which the premises are wholly or partly situated;

(g)   the body designated in writing by the Licensing Authority responsible for advising the Authority about the protection of children from harm;

(h)   the commissioners of HM Revenue and Customs; and

(i) any other person prescribed by regulations made by the Secretary of State.

To date, no regulations have been made prescribing other parties as responsible authorities.

An interested party is a person who:

(a) lives sufficiently close to the premises to be likely to be affected by the authorised activities;

(b) has business interests that might be affected by the authorised activities; or

(c) represents persons who satisfy (a) or (b).

Paragraph 8.11 of the Gambling Commission Guidance states "interested parties can be persons who are democratically elected such as councillors and MPs. Where appropriate this will include county, parish, and town councillors. Other than these persons, authorities should require written evidence that a person "represents" someone who either lives sufficiently close to the premises to be likely to be affected by the authorised activities and/or has business interests that might be affected by the authorised activities. A letter from one of these persons requesting the representation is sufficient."

Despite this paragraph in the Guidance, if a councillor made a representation who did not live near the relevant premises and was unable to show that they had been requested by a constituent who lived sufficiently close to the premises to be likely to be affected by the activities, the member could be open to a challenge that they were not representing their constituent but were merely acting on their own behalf. It could then be argued that the member was putting forward their own personal views which might be contrary to the views of their electorate. If a councillor does have concerns about an application and wishes to make a representation, it is very likely that some constituents share the concerns. In these circumstances, it would seem very easy for a councillor to obtain a letter from a constituent asking the member to represent them. This would then prevent an applicant challenging the member's representation.

Representations

If representations are made, there must be a hearing before the Licensing Committee unless the representations are withdrawn or the Licensing Authority determine that the representations are:

(a)   vexatious;

(b)   frivolous; or

(c)   will certainly not influence the Authority's determination of the application.

Ground (c) would enable a Licensing Authority to reject a representation in circumstances where an issue was raised by an interested party or responsible authority which did relate to one of the objectives but was so minor or vague it would not influence the Authority to refuse the application or consider attaching conditions, e.g. a representation to an application for a new betting shop on the grounds that "18 months ago I saw someone who might have been under 18 coming out of the applicant's betting shop in another town".

If the Licensing Authority decide that a representation falls within one of the above categories and intend to make a decision on the application without a hearing, they must, as soon as is reasonably practicable, notify any person who made a representation (section 162).

Representations must be made to the Licensing Authority within 28 days of the date of the application being made (Regulation 15(2), Gambling Act 2005 (Premises Licences and Provisional Statements) Regulations 2007). Does this mean a representation made after the 28 days must be rejected? The answer is "no" following the House of Lords decision in *Belfast City Council v Miss Behavin' Ltd* (2007) LLR 12. As a result of this, it is clear that, provided there has been a valid representation made within the 28-day period, further representations received after the 28 days may be considered at the discretion of the Licensing Authority. They must not automatically be rejected because they are late.

The *Miss Behavin' Ltd* case involved an application for a sex shop licence under the Local Government (Miscellaneous Provisions) Act 1982. The wording in the 1982 Act regarding representations being made within 28 days is the same as in the 2005 Act. The House of Lords held that the provisions regarding objections (representations in the 2005 Act) concern the position of the party objecting. If a party did not comply within the 28 days, they could not complain if their objection was rejected. However, the wording of the Act did not prohibit the Authority from taking into account all relevant matters, whether they be received early or late. The Court also held that it would be very strange if the legislation, designed to enable the Authority to carry on its business in an orderly and expeditious manner, had the effect of requiring the Authority to shut its eyes to facts which it considered relevant to its decision. If an Authority received a late objection that was relevant, there could be circumstances where the Authority's failure to take it into account would itself be judicially reviewable. The Court then went on to say that there could be circumstances where it was right to disregard a late representation if it was intentionally last minute or if it was received so late that taking it into account would lead to unfairness to the applicant.

The effect of the decision is that late objections could, but need not, be taken into account. However, great care should be taken in rejecting a late representation. It is suggested that the following procedure should be considered when a late representation is received which is relevant:

(a)   consider how late the representation is. Is it so late there would be unfairness to the applicant to take it into account? If the answer is "no", then:

(b)   send a copy to the applicant and ask for any observations;

(c)   if the applicant does not object, include the representation with the papers for the hearing;

(d)   if the applicant does object but it is still considered the representation is relevant and contains information which is relevant for the members to take into account when making their decision, do not include the document with the paperwork but take copies to the hearing where:

(e)   the applicant is asked for their views as to why it should not be taken into account;

(f)   views as to why it should be taken into account are then considered;

(g)   the members then decide whether or not to take the late representation into account. Their task is to balance the prejudice to the person making the representation of not taking it into account, against the prejudice to the applicant of taking the representation into account;

(h)   if the decision is made to take the late representation into account, the applicant is offered the opportunity of an adjournment to consider the document.

The hearing

The Government have made hearing regulations regarding the procedure to be followed by the Authority at the hearing of an application.

The Gambling Act 2005 (Proceedings of Licensing Committees and Sub-Committees) (Premises Licences and Provisional Statements) (England and Wales) Regulations 2007 provide that Authorities will have to serve a notice of the hearing on the applicant and anyone who has made representations (Regulation 5). The notice will set out the rights of the parties, the fact the hearing can proceed in their absence, the procedure to be followed at the hearing, the time limit by which a potential attendee should indicate whether or not they are going to attend the meeting, how and within what timescale a party should inform the Committee whether or not they are going to be represented and/or call witnesses, the time limit within which they should withdraw representations if they wish to do so and any matters upon which the Authority would like clarification. Regulation 5(2)(c) provides that, in the ordinary course of events, the notice of the meeting must be received no later than ten working days before the first day of the hearing.

In addition to the above points, the notice should also inform the parties that all relevant representations will be made available to all parties should they wish to have them.

Regulation 4 requires the hearing to be held "as soon as reasonably practicable" after the end of the 28 days for people to make representations. It is considered good practice to have a hearing within 20 working days of the end of the 28-day representation period. If it is not possible to have a hearing within 20 working days, a note should be kept of the reason why the hearing was not held and a hearing arranged as soon as possible. A situation where it may be appropriate to delay having a hearing would be if the police made a representation and were still having discussions with the applicant to see if their concerns could be resolved without the need for a hearing.

At the hearing, the Committee must ensure that each party is given the opportunity to address the Committee, call witnesses and provide further information on any matter on which the Committee has indicated they want further clarification (Regulation 9(3)). The Committee must also permit any party to question another party on any relevant matter or any representations that have been made, where the Committee considers it is appropriate to do so, and the Committee must take into account any documentary evidence produced before the hearing or at the hearing with the consent of all other parties attending (Regulation 9(4)).

There has been some discussion about Regulation 9(4). In some cases, applicants have been objecting to a Committee taking into account information produced at a hearing. They have argued that the Committee can only take into account information produced at the hearing if all of the parties agree; if one party objects, it cannot be considered. This view seems to be contrary to a fair hearing. If information is produced at a hearing, it is relevant to the matter to be determined and, if one of the parties objects to it being taken into account, it is suggested that the Committee should:

(a) ask the party objecting why the information should not be taken into account;

(b) ask the party producing the information why it should be taken into account;

(c) consider the prejudice to the party objecting of taking the information into account;

(d) consider the prejudice to the party producing the information of not taking it into account;

(e) decide whether or not to consider the information, giving reasons for the decision.

As a judge said in similar circumstances, "The Committee's task is to find the least unfair course" (*R(T) v Head Teacher of Elliot School and Others* (2003) ELR 160).

Regulation 9(5) provides that the hearing must be conducted so that it takes the form of a discussion led by the relevant Committee and cross-examination should not be permitted unless the Committee considers it to be required for the members to properly consider the matter.

This Regulation seems rather strange and unneccessary as the Authority has to lay down a procedure to be followed at a hearing. The Committee must ensure there is a fair hearing for all parties which means giving everyone the opportunity to say what they want to say, provided that it is relevant to the matter to be determined. Reading the Regulations together, the intention seems to be that there must be a laid-down procedure that the parties are notified of before the hearing. However, the Committee can depart from the procedure if they consider it is necessary to do so, e.g. a party has presented their case and later in the hearing remember an important point they forgot to mention: the party should be given the opportunity to put forward the information provided the other parties can comment on the new information.

The reference in Regulation 9(5) to no cross-examination does not stop a party asking questions. There is a big difference between asking questions to clarify points and cross-examining to try to show someone is not telling the truth.

Decisions should be made within five working days following the last day on which the hearing was held. In addition, Licensing Authorities should keep records of the hearing for six years.

Regulation 7 enables a Committee to adjourn a hearing. Regulation 8 provides that the hearing must be held in public unless the Committee decides that to do so would not be in the public interest. Hearings under the Gambling Act 2005 are outside the Local Government Act 1972. As a result, if a Committee decides to exclude the public, they can do so for any reason they consider to be in the public interest.

Determination

On considering the application, the Licensing Authority, whether at the hearing or not, shall:

(a)   grant it; or

(b)   reject it (section 163).

Under section 169, the Authority has power to attach conditions when granting a premises licence.

Whether an application is granted, granted subject to conditions or rejected, the Authority must give notice of the decision to:

(a)   the applicant;

(b)   the Gambling Commission;

(c)   any person who made representations;

(d)   the police;

(e)   the commissioners of HM Revenue and Customs.

The forms the Licensing Authority must use to notify the above parties of their decision are prescribed in Schedule 7 to the Gambling Act 2005 (Premises Licences and Provisional Statements) Regulations 2007.

Conditions

Under section 167, the Secretary of State can provide for a specified condition to be attached to premises licences Mandatory Conditions. In addition, the Secretary of State can by regulations prescribe for a specified condition to be attached to any premises licence unless excluded by the Authority who issued the licence default conditions. For more information, see the section on Premises Licence Conditions on page 121.

Fees

The Gambling (Premises Licence Fees) (England and Wales) Regulations 2007 set out the maximum fees to be paid for premises licences. Licensing Authorities have a discretion to set the fees up to the prescribed maximum but subject to cost recovery. However, if an Authority is rated as good or excellent in their audit commission assessment, they have a discretion to set the fees outside the prescribed bands but again subject to the level of fee equating to cost recovery.

The maximum fee for a fast track application is £300.

Section 184 requires annual fees to be paid to the Authority and the premises licence can be cancelled in the event of the annual fee not being paid, unless failure to pay was due to an administrative oversight.

The levels of fees prescribed are presented in the table on the following pages.

TABLE OF MAXIMUM FEES

Class of premises licence	Maximum conversion application fee for non-fast track application	Maximum non-conversion application fee in respect of provisional statement premises	Maximum non-conversion application fee in respect of other premises	Maximum annual fee	Maximum fee for application to vary licence	Maximum fee for application to transfer a licence	Maximum fee for application for reinstatement of a licence	Maximum fee for application for provisional statement
Regional casino premises licence	£8,000	£15,000	£15,000	£7,500	£6,500	£6,500	£15,000	
Large casino premises licence	£5,000	£10,000	£10,000	£5,000	£2,150	£2,150	£10,000	
Small casino premises licence	£3,000	£8,000	£5,000	£4,000	£1,800	£1,800	£8,000	
Converted casino premises licence	£2,000	£3,000	£2,000	£1,350	£1,350			

Bingo premises licence	£1,750	£1,200	£3,500	£1,000	£1,750	£1,200	£1,200	£3,500
Adult gaming centre premises licence	£1,000	£1,200	£2,000	£1,000	£1,000	£1,200	£1,200	£2,000
Betting premises (track) licence	£1,250	£950	£2,500	£1,000	£1,250	£950	£950	£2,500
Family entertainment centre premises licence	£1,000	£950	£2,000	£750	£1,000	£850	£850	£2,000
Betting premises (other) licence	£1,500	£1,200	£3,000	£600	£1,500	£1,200	£1,200	£3,000

ISSUES RELATING TO PREMISES LICENCES

Availability of licence for inspection

Under section 185, the holder of a premises licence must keep the licence on the premises and it must be available for inspection by:

1. A police constable.

2. An enforcement officer.

3. An authorised local authority officer.

In addition, a summary of the premises licence must be displayed at the premises.

Change of circumstances

Under section 186, if the holder of a premises licence ceases to reside or attend at the address specified in the licence, he/she must, as soon as is reasonably practicable:

(a) notify the Licensing Authority; and

(b) inform the Licensing Authority of a home or business address at which he/she resides or attends.

The Secretary of State has power to make regulations requiring the holder of a premises licence to notify the Licensing Authority of any change of circumstances of a prescribed kind in relation to him/her or to an authorised activity and to give the Licensing Authority prescribed details of the change. Where such notification is accompanied by the licence, the Licensing Authority must make necessary alterations and return the licence to the licensee. No regulations had been made at the time of publication of this book.

Variation of licence

By virtue of section 187, the holder of a premises licence may apply to vary the licence at any time by:

(a) adding, amending or removing an authorised activity;

(b) amending another detail of the licence;

(c) excluding certain conditions; or

(d) adding, amending or removing conditions imposed or excluded by the Licensing Authority.

When making regulations which relate to an application for a premises licence, the Secretary of State may make:

(a) provisions which apply only in the case of an application for variation;

(b) provisions which do not apply in the case of an application for variation;

(c) different provisions in relation to an application for variation from those made in relation to an application for a premises licence;

(d) different provisions in relation to applications for variations of different kinds.

The regulations made under this provision are the Gambling Act 2005 (Premises Licences and Provisional Statements) Regulations 2007.

Any application for a variation must be accompanied by a statement of the variation sought and also the licence or a statement explaining why it is not reasonably practicable to produce the licence. If the variation will mean a change to the plan submitted when the application was made for the premises licence, a new plan must be submitted with the variation application.

When granting an application for a variation, the Licensing Authority must specify a time when the variation shall begin to have effect and may make transitional provisions.

Transfer

Section 188 enables a person to apply for a transfer of a premises licence. The application must specify the time when the transfer is to take effect and be accompanied by a written statement from the existing licensee consenting to the transfer. The Licensing Authority must grant the application unless they think it would be wrong to do so having regard to representations made.

If an application for a transfer of a licence states that the applicant has failed to contact the licensee, having taken all reasonable steps to do so, the Authority has the discretion to deal with the transfer in the absence of the written consent of the present licensee.

Duration of licence

By virtue of section 191, the Secretary of State has power to make regulations prescribing the length of the life of a premises licence. The regulations may also make provisions regarding the renewal of such a licence. If no regulations are made then any premises licence will be of unlimited duration. No regulations have been made so far.

Surrender/lapse

Under section 192, the holder of a licence can surrender it. In addition, if the annual fee is not paid, the Licensing Authority has a duty to revoke the licence unless they think the failure to pay is due to an administrative error.

By virtue of section 194, a licence shall lapse if:

    (a)   the licensee dies;

    (b)   the licensee becomes, in the opinion of the Licensing Authority, incapable of carrying on the licensed activities by reason of mental or physical incapacity;

(c)　the licensee becomes bankrupt;

(d)　sequestration of the licensee's estate is awarded under section 12(1) of the Bankruptcy (Scotland) Act 1985.

Should the licensee cease to exist or go into liquidation, the licence will automatically lapse. When the Authority becomes aware that a premises licence has lapsed they must, as soon as is reasonably practicable, notify:

(a)　the Gambling Commission;

(b)　the chief officer of police; and

(c)　the commissioners of HM Revenue and Customs (section 194(3)).

Where a licence lapses because of the death, incapacity or bankruptcy of the licensee then, during the period of six months beginning with the date of the lapse, a person may apply for the licence to be reinstated (section 195).

Review of licence

Under section 197, a responsible authority under section 157, or interested party, may apply at any time for a review of a licence. The application must be made in the prescribed form and manner. The Secretary of State has made regulations regarding the procedure to be followed, including specifying timescales within which certain notices and/or representations can be made.

An application for a review can be rejected if the Licensing Authority thinks the grounds on which it is made:

(a)　do not raise an issue relevant to the guidance, code of practice, policy or licensing objectives;

(b)　are frivolous;

(c)　are vexatious;

(d)   will certainly not cause the Authority to wish to take any action in respect of the licence;

(e)   are substantially the same as the grounds specified in an earlier application for a review of the licence; or

(f)   are substantially the same as representations made in relation to the application for the premises licence.

In considering whether or not to reject an application under grounds (e) or (f), the Licensing Authority must consider the length of time that has passed since the making of the earlier application for a review or since the making of representations in respect of the application for the licence (section 198).

Initiation of review by Licensing Authority

Section 200 provides that, where a review is initiated by the Licensing Authority, the Authority may:

(a)   review a particular class of premises licences, to assess the use of those premises or the arrangements made to ensure compliance with licence conditions (subsection (1)); or

(b)   review a particular premises licence, where it suspects that the premises have not been used in accordance with a condition of a licence, or if it thinks that a review would be appropriate for any other reason. Before conducting such a review, the Licensing Authority must give notice of its intention to review the licence to the affected licensee, and also publish its intention.

The Secretary of State may specify the form and manner of the notice of intention to review, and also the period of time within which notice is to be given. Where such regulations are made, they must specify a period of time within which representations about the review may be made by the licensee, a responsible authority or an interested party (Gambling Act 2005 (Premises Licences) (Review) Regulations 2007). If a Licensing Authority decides to commence a review under section 200, they must serve notice on the holder of the premises licence, each of the responsible authorities and any interested party. The notice must be given to the responsible authorities and interested parties within seven days of the notice being given to the holder of the premises licence. The notice must give these parties 28 days to make representations. The Licensing Authority must also publish notice of their intention to hold a review, either in a local newpaper, local newsletter or circular or similar document, or on the Authority's internet website and display a notice at a place as near as reasonably practicable to the premises that is the subject of the review where it can be read by members of the public (Regulation 8).

If the Authority fails to give proper notice of the intention to hold a review to either the holder of the premises licence or a responsible authority, or fails to properly publish notice of the intention to hold a review, the Authority can correct the error but the 28 days for people to make representations will only start on the day when the error is corrected (Regulations 9, 10 and 11).

Where the Licensing Authority has granted an application for a review, or has given notice of its intention to initiate a review, it must review the licence as soon as reasonably practicable (after the period for giving representations has expired) in order to determine what, if any, action should be taken (section 201).

Procedure for a review

The Gambling Act 2005 (Premises Licences) (Review) Regulations 2007 set out the procedure to be followed in connection with a review under the 2005 Act. The

Regulations prescribe the application form to be completed by someone wanting a review. The person applying for the review must, within seven days of the date on which the application for the review is made, serve on the holder of the premises licence and all the responsible authorities notice that application for the review has been made (Regulation 4). If a responsible authority applies for a review, they do not have to serve themselves with a copy of the review application.

Following receipt of an application for a review, the Licensing Authority must display a notice as near as reasonably practicable to the premises the subject of the review, where it can be read conveniently by members of the public, and publish a notice in a local newspaper or newsletter, circular or similar document or on the Authority's internet website. The notice near the premises must be displayed for 28 days starting seven days after the date on which the application for the review was made (Regulation 5).

If the applicant for a review does not serve the holder of the premises licence or a responsible authority with the relevant notice, the application for the review does not automatically become void. Regulation 6 provides that, when the applicant becomes aware of the error, they can serve the notice on the person who was not originally served. That person then has 28 days from being served to make a representation and the Licensing Authority cannot hold a hearing until that time has passed.

If the Licensing Authority fails to publish a notice of an application for a review in the appropriate form or manner and within the required period, Regulation 7 enables the Authority to correct this error by publishing the appropriate notice. However, the period of 28 days for representations to be made starts on the day on which the correct notice is published.

In conducting the review, the Licensing Authority must hold a hearing unless the applicant for the review and any person who made representations have consented to the hearing being waived; or the Licensing Authority considers that all the representations made following notice of the review are frivolous, vexatious or will not influence their decision.

Action following review
Under section 202, following a review, a Licensing Authority may:

(a) suspend (for a period not exceeding three months) or revoke a licence; or

(b) amend, add or exclude conditions attached to the licence. This includes reinstating a condition imposed under section 168 that they had previously excluded under section 169. For example, where the Authority had excluded the default condition that a betting shop may only open between 7.00am and 10.00pm to allow the shop to be open 24 hours and the police ask for a review, the Authority has the power to reimpose the default condition.

When determining what, if any, action under section 202(1) to take, the Licensing Authority must take into account representations made before or during the hearing, and the grounds specified in any application for a review made by a responsible Authority or an interested party.

Determination
Following the review of a licence, the Licensing Authority must notify the licensee, the applicant for a review, the Gambling Commission, any person who made representations, the police and HM Revenue and Customs of their decision as soon as possible after it has been made. The Authority must give reasons for their decision. (Section 203.)

Appeals

There is a right of appeal to the magistrates' court from any determination made by the Licensing Authority in connection with a review. This means that the holder of a licence can appeal, as well as the person who applied for the review, anyone who made representations to the review from following its being advertised and the Gambling Commission. The Gambling Commission may lodge an appeal against the decision of the Licensing Authority, even if they were not a party to the review hearing.

PREMISES LICENCE CONDITIONS

Mandatory conditions

The Secretary of State has made regulations specifying mandatory conditions (Gambling Act 2005 (Mandatory and Default Conditions) (England and Wales) Regulations 2007). These must be imposed on a premises licence and cannot be altered.

As a result, the following conditions will apply to all gambling premises licences:

1. Lottery products, including National Lottery products, may not be sold on the premises.

2. A summary of terms and conditions of the premises licence must be prominently displayed.

3. The layout of the premises must be maintained in accordance with the plan.

Casinos

- The principal entrance to a casino must be from the street (defined as any bridge, road, lane, footway, subway, square, court, alley or passage – including passages through enclosed premises such as shopping malls) whether a thoroughfare or not.

- There must be no access to a casino from premises wholly or mainly used by children and young people.

- There must be a gap of at least two metres between a gaming table and any other gambling equipment.

- No more than 40 separate player positions are allowed at wholly automated versions of real games of chance ("automated gaming tables").

- The rules of each type of casino game must be displayed prominently, either on signs or customer leaflets.

Regional casinos

- A notice must be prominently displayed at every entrance to the gambling area stating that no-one under 18 is permitted to enter that part of the premises.

- The gambling area of the regional casino should not be capable of being seen from any part of the premises to which children or young people have access.

Layout of new casinos

- Casinos must provide the following minimum table gaming area:

  - Small casinos: a minimum of 500m^2;

  - Large casinos: a minimum of 1,000m^2;

  - Regional casinos: a minimum of 1,000m^2.

- Only table gaming may take place in the table gaming areas of casinos.

- No area counting towards the minimum table gaming area may comprise less than 12.5% of the total minimum table gaming area for that category of casino.

- No other gambling facilities may be situated within two metres of any ordinary table game.

For the purposes of these conditions, table games are defined as:

(i)   ordinary table games, i.e. gaming tables which facilitate the playing of casino games such as card games, dice games, roulette, etc.;

(ii) tables operated by employees but on which customers place stakes on automated terminals;

(iii) wholly automated tables of the sort permitted by virtue of section 235(2)(i) of the Act.

- The following minimum non-gambling areas must be offered:

  – Regional casinos: 1,500m^2;

  – Large casinos: 500m^2;

  – Small casinos: 250m^2.

- No gambling facilities may be offered in the non-gambling area.

- The non-gambling area may consist of one or more areas.

- The area must be readily available to customers (i.e. offices, kitchen areas, staff areas will not count).

- The area must include recreational facilities for casino customers which are available for use when the casino is open; where there is more than one area, each area must contain recreational facilities.

- The area may include, but should not consist exclusively of, lavatories and lobby areas.

Converted casino licences

- Casinos with converted licences, and which have a gambling area of over 200m^2, must offer a minimum non-gambling area equivalent to at least 10% of the total gambling area.

Adult gaming centres and family entertainment centres

Adult gaming centres must display a sign stating that no-one under 18 is permitted to enter the premises.

- The consumption of alcohol is prohibited in adult gaming centres and family entertainment centres.

Betting shops (other than tracks)

- Must display a sign stating that no-one under 18 is permitted to enter the premises.

- No apparatus for making information or other material available in the form of sounds or visual images may be used on the licensed premises, except where the matter seen or heard is a sporting event and bets may have been affected on the premises in relation to that event. Betting operator-owned TV channels will be permitted.

- No music, dancing or other entertainment is permitted.

- The consumption of alcohol is prohibited.

- The only publications that may be sold on the premises are racing periodicals or specialist betting publications.

ATMs

- ATMs (cash machines) in casinos, betting shops, bingo halls, adult gaming centres or family entertainment centres must be positioned so that customers must cease to gamble at tables or gaming machines in order to use them.

Betting machines

- There must be no more than 40 betting positions at betting machines on tracks and the new casinos.

Access

- There can be no direct access from one premises licensed under the Gambling Act 2005 to which under-18s are not permitted to another such premises where under-18s are not permitted.

Over-18 areas within family entertainment centres and bingo halls that admit under-18s must be separated by a barrier with notices displayed prominently stating that under-18s are not allowed in that area and they must have adequate supervision in place to ensure that children and young people are not able to access these areas or the Category B or C machines. Supervision may be done either by placing the terminals within the line of sight of an official of the betting operator or via monitored CCTV.

There should be no access to a betting premises from another premises which undertakes a commercial activity (except from other premises with a betting premises licence, including tracks). In addition, the entrance to a betting shop should be from the street (defined as any bridge, road, lane, footway, subway, square, court, alley or passage and including passages through enclosed premises such as shopping malls) whether a thoroughfare or not.

Default conditions

The Secretary of State has made the Gambling Act 2005 (Mandatory and Default Conditions) (England and Wales) Regulations 2007 prescribing default conditions. These must be attached to a premises licence unless an applicant applies for them to be removed or varied.

The default conditions relate to opening hours:

- Casinos: no gambling between 6.00am and noon.

- Betting offices: no gambling between 6.00pm and 7.00am.

- Bingo: no gambling between midnight and 9.00am.

Conditions imposed or excluded by the Licensing Authority

The Licensing Authority can attach any condition they consider appropriate, having regard to the licensing objectives, the guidance and their policy. In addition, they can exclude or vary a default condition. However, before attaching a condition, the Authority should tell the applicant what condition or conditions they are considering attaching to the premises licence and give reasons, and give the applicant the opportunity of a hearing. If an applicant informs the Authority they have no objection to the proposed condition or conditions being attached, there does not seem to be any reason why officers should not issue the premises licence with the conditions attached.

If a Licensing Authority does attach or exclude a condition, they will have to give reasons as to why when they notify people of their decision.

Membership

A premises licence may not be subject to a condition requiring all or part of the premises to be operated or carried on as a club or subject to any other membership requirement, or a condition restricting use of any part of the premises with reference to membership.

Stakes

A Licensing Authority cannot impose conditions on a premises licence regarding limits on how much people can stake, the amount of any fees that can be paid, winnings or maximum or minimum prizes.

APPEALS

There are various rights of appeal in the legislation. If an application is rejected, the applicant can appeal against that decision. Where a licence is granted subject to conditions, a person who made representations can appeal, as can the applicant (section 206(1) and (2)).

Where a Licensing Authority take action as a result of a review of a licence, or determine to take no action as a result of a review, the following may appeal:

(a)   the licensee;

(b)   a person who made representations in relation to the review;

(c)   the person who applied for the review; and

(d)   the Gambling Commission (section 206(3)).

The appeal is made to the magistrates' court for the area in which the premises are wholly or partially situated.

The magistrates may:

(a)   dismiss the appeal;

(b)   substitute for the decision appealed against a decision that the Licensing Authority could have made;

(c)   remit the case to the Licensing Authority to decide in accordance with a direction of the court;

(d)   make an order as to costs (section 207(3)).

The only further appeal is to the High Court on a point of law (section 209).

Any appeal must be started within the 21-day period beginning on the day on which the appellant receives notice of the decision against which they are appealing (section 207(1)).

VEHICLES AND VESSELS

Section 211 provides that premises licenses may be granted to passenger vessels but cannot be granted to vehicles.

A "vehicle" includes:

(a) a train;

(b) an aircraft;

(c) a sea plane; and

(d) an amphibious vehicle other than a hovercraft.

A "vessel" includes:

(a) anything, other than a sea-plane or an amphibious vehicle, designed or adapted for navigation or other use in, on or over water;

(b) a hovercraft;

(c) anything, or any part of any place, situated in or on water.

Permits under Schedule 10 (family entertainment centre gaming machine permits), Schedule 12 (club gaming permits and club machine permits) and Schedule 14 (prize gaming permits) cannot be granted to vessels or vehicles. Permits under Schedule 13 (licensed premises gaming machine permits) can be issued for vehicles and vessels as long as they hold the appropriate licence under the Licensing Act 2003.

A vessel that is on a journey which has taken it or is intending to take it into international waters is exempt from licensing (section 359).

TEMPORARY USE OF PREMISES

A person holding an operating licence can serve on the Licensing Authority a notice regarding the temporary use of premises for:

(a)   a casino;

(b)   facilities for the playing of bingo;

(c)   use of a gaming machine;

(d)   other facilities for gaming; or

(e)   facilities for betting.

The Secretary of State has power to make regulations prescribing the activities that can be carried out under the terms of a temporary use notice (section 215(2)). The Gambling Act 2005 (Temporary Use Notices) Regulations 2007 provide that the only gambling that may be played under a temporary use notice is equal chance gaming. By section 8 of the Gambling Act 2005, gaming is equal chance if:

(a)   does not involve playing or staking against a bank; and

(b)   the chances are equally favourable to all participants.

This means that, in reality, it would be difficult to hold a casino under a temporary use notice as most of the games in a casino, e.g. poker, involve playing against a banker.

Before a temporary use notice can be served, the person intending to serve it must have an operating licence authorising him/her to carry out the activities specified in the temporary use notice (section 215(3)).

The notice will have to be in the prescribed form and set out details of:

(a)   the activity to be carried on;

(b)   the premises where they will be carried on;

(c)   the period of time during which the notice is to have effect;

(d)   the times of day during that period at which the activity is to be carried on;

(e)   any periods during the previous 12 months during which a temporary use notice has had effect in respect of the premises; and

(f)   the specified date on which the notice is given (section 216).

The "previous 12 months" means the period of 12 months ending with the last day of the period specified in the notice for the activity to take place (section 216(3)).

A set of premises may not be used for gambling under a temporary use notice for more than 21 days in any 12-month period. However, a set of premises may be the subject of more than one temporary use notice in a period of 12 months, provided that the total number of days does not exceed 21 (section 218).

If a temporary use notice is served on the Licensing Authority and its effect would be that the premises would be used for more than 21 days in a 12-month period, the Licensing Authority must serve a counter notice (section 218(3)).

A temporary use notice must be given at least three months before the first day specified in the notice for the use of the premises (section 219(2)). In addition, a copy of the notice must be served on:

(a)   the Gambling Commission;

(b)   the chief officer of police;

(c)   the commissioners of HM Revenue and Customs
       (section 219(4)).

If premises are situated within two Licensing Authority
areas, the notice must be served on both authorities. As
soon as practicable after receiving the notice, the Licensing
Authority must send a written acknowledgement to the
person who gave the notice (section 220).

Anyone giving a temporary use notice must ensure that it is
received by the Authority and the other parties who have to
be served, within the period of seven days beginning with
the date specified in the notice as the date on which the
notice is given (section 221(4)).

Any person served with a temporary use notice can object
to its provisions by giving notice to the Licensing Authority
setting out their reasons for objecting. If such a notice is
served, the Licensing Authority must arrange a hearing,
unless all the parties agree a hearing is unnecessary. Any
party served with a copy of the temporary use notice that
wishes to object must give a notice of objection within 14
days beginning with the date on which the temporary use
notice is given (section 221(4)). The temporary use notice
must specify the date on which the notice is given.

Where a notice of objection has been served to a temporary
use notice and there has been a hearing and the decision is
that the notice should not have effect or should have effect
only with modification, the Licensing Authority must serve a
counter notice. The counter notice must be in the prescribed
form and may provide for the temporary use notice:

(a)   not to have effect;

(b)   to have effect only in respect of a specified
       activity;

(c)   to have effect only in respect of activity carried

on during a specified period of time or at specified times of day;

(d)   to have effect subject to compliance with a specified condition (section 224(3)).

If the Licensing Authority determine not to give a counter notice to a temporary use notice, they must give notice of that determination to the person serving the notice and everyone else who received a copy of the notice (section 225).

If the Licensing Authority give a counter notice or make a decision not to serve a counter notice, the person serving the notice or anyone who is entitled to receive a copy of the notice can appeal to the magistrates' court. When dealing with an appeal, the magistrates' court may:

(a)   dismiss the appeal;

(b)   direct the Licensing Authority to take action of a specified kind;

(c)   remit the case to the Licensing Authority to decide in accordance with a direction of the court;

(d)   make an order about costs (section 226(6)).

The person who gave the temporary use notice can appeal against a decision of the Authority, as can any person who is entitled to receive a copy of the temporary use notice (section 226(2)).

If no objection has been made to a temporary use notice within 14 days of the notice being given, the Licensing Authority must endorse a copy of it and return it, as soon as is reasonably practicable, to the person giving the notice (section 227(2)). If a notice of objection is pending at the end of the 14-day period then, as soon as is reasonably practicable after the completion of the proceedings, the

Licensing Authority must, unless they give a counter notice, endorse a copy of the notice and return it to the person who gave the notice (section 227(3)).

If a notice is given to the Licensing Authority within the 14-day period, the Authority must complete the proceedings, before the end of a 6-week period beginning with the date on which they receive the notice (section 228(1)).

The person who served a temporary use notice must arrange for a copy of it to be displayed prominently on the premises at any time when an activity is being carried on under the notice (section 229(1)(a)). They must also arrange for a copy of the notice to be produced, on request, to:

(a)   a constable;

(b)   an enforcement officer;

(c)   an authorised local authority officer;

(d)   an officer of HM Revenue and Customs (section 229(1)(b)).

The Licensing Authority must maintain a register of temporary use notices that is available for inspection at all reasonable times (section 234).

Under section 231, a temporary use notice:

(a)   may not be given in respect of a vehicle or part of a vehicle;

(b)   may be given in respect of all or part of a passenger vessel;

(c)   may be given in respect of all or part of a vessel situated at a fixed place in or on water; and

(d)   may not be given in respect of all or part of a vessel to which neither (b) or (c) applies.

Occasional use notices

Where there is betting on a track, i.e. a racecourse, dog track or other sporting place and betting is carried out on eight days or less in a calendar year, betting may be permitted by an occasional use notice without there being in force a full premises licence (section 39). However, anyone actually taking the bets must have the appropriate operating licence.

An occasional use notice must specify the day on which it has effect and must be served on the Licensing Authority and the police.

Part 4
GAMBLING LEGISLATION –
GENERAL

ADVERTISING

Meaning of "advertising"

Section 327 sets out what it means to advertise gambling for the purposes of the Act. The definition is very broad and covers anything which is done to encourage people to take advantage of facilities for gambling (subsection (1)(a)). It also covers bringing information about gambling facilities to people's attention with a view to increasing the use of those facilities (subsection (1)(b)). As well as covering the activities of those who act with the specific intention of encouraging the use of facilities for gambling as described in subsection (1)(a) and (b), the definition also provides for the advertising of gambling to include those who participate in or facilitate such activities. Advertising includes entering into arrangements such as sponsorship or brand-sharing agreements.

Regulations

Section 328 gives the Secretary of State power to make regulations controlling the form, content, timing and location of advertisements for gambling, including requirements for specified words to be included in advertisements. A specific duty is imposed on the Secretary of State to have regard to the need to protect children and other vulnerable persons from being harmed or exploited by gambling.

It is an offence under this section to contravene a requirement of the regulations and any person guilty of an offence shall be liable on summary conviction to imprisonment for a term not exceeding 51 weeks (six months for Scotland), a fine not exceeding level 5 on the standard scale, or both. An offence committed under this section shall be treated as a continuing offence which means that an offence shall be committed on each day during any period that the regulations are contravened.

Unlawful gambling

Section 330 makes it an offence to advertise unlawful gambling, i.e. advertising gambling facilities where the necessary licences have not been obtained.

On conviction, a person can be jailed for up to 51 weeks and also subject to a fine up to level 5.

Offences under section 330 are continuing offences. The effect of this is that an offence is committed on each day during which the unlawful gambling is advertised.

Foreign gambling

Section 331 makes it an offence to advertise non-EEA (or "foreign") gambling.

If gambling takes place in a non-European state or is remote gambling not controlled by any European state, it is regarded as foreign gambling.

The penalty for breaching section 331 is the same as for section 330.

Non-remote advertising

Regulations can be made controlling non-remote advertising, e.g. advertisement hoardings (section 332).

Remote advertising

If advertising of gambling is carried out by remote means, e.g. television, the advertising will have to fulfil three tests (section 333).

The first test is that advertising must be intended to come to the attention of people in Great Britain.

The second test is that the advertising must comply with any European directives where they are applicable, e.g. Directive 89/552/EEC (television without frontiers) and Directive 2000/31/EEC (properly functioning internal markets).

Section 331 of the 2007 Act makes it unlawful to advertise foreign gambling other than a lottery. Foreign gambling is defined in section 331(2). Non-remote gambling constitutes foreign gambling if it takes place in a non-EEA state and remote gambling constitutes foreign gambling if none of the arrangements for it are subject to the laws of an EEA state. Gibraltar is treated as an EEA state for these purposes. In addition, the Secretary of State can specify that a country or place is to be treated as an EEA state for the purposes of the definition of foreign gambling. Regulation 2 of the Gambling Act 2005 (Advertising of Foreign Gambling) Regulations 2007 specifies the Isle of Alderney as a place which is to be treated as an EEA state but only in so far as the legislation applies to remote gambling. The section 331 offence will still apply in respect of advertising non-remote gambling services. Regulation 3 specifies that the Isle of Man is to be treated as an EEA state for the purposes of both remote and non-remote gambling which takes place in a casino. The section 331 offence will still apply in respect of advertising non-remote gambling services other than those which take place in a casino.

The final test is that the gambling must take place in Great Britain and, if it is remote gambling, at least one piece of the gambling equipment must be situated in Great Britain. A code of practice in connection with gambling has been issued containing the following points.

- Gambling products, except bingo and the lottery, should not be advertised on television before 9.00pm.

- Sports betting advertising will be allowed around televised sporting events before the watershed. Televised dancing and celebrity ice-skating competitions do not count as sporting events.

- Logos and other gambling promotional material should not appear on commercial merchandise which is designed for use by children, such as replica sports shirts.

- Post-watershed advertisements must not portray, encourage or condone gambling behaviour that is socially irresponsible or could lead to financial harm.

- Advertisements must not link gambling to seduction, sexual success or enhanced attractiveness.

- Advertisements must not be directed at children or feature people who are, or who appear to be, under 25.

- Advertisements must not suggest that gambling can be a solution to money problems.

- Print advertisements must include an approved message.

- Advertisements must include a reference to www.gambleaware.co.uk.

ENFORCEMENT

Enforcement officers

The Gambling Commission have power to appoint enforcement officers. They may also appoint people who are not employees of the Commission. (Section 303.)

Authorised persons

Licensing Authorities can appoint officers of their Authority as authorised persons to carry out enforcement duties under the 2005 Act. An inspector appointed under the Health & Safety at Work etc Act 1974 is automatically an authorised person. (Section 304.)

Compliance

Section 305 confers express powers on constables, authorised persons and enforcement officers to undertake activities to assess whether a provision of the Act is being complied with or whether an offence is being committed. The powers include the ability to ask a child or young person to make a "test purchase" in respect of gambling.

Rights of entry

Suspected offence

If the police or Gambling Commission consider an offence is being committed on a premises, or is about to be committed, they have an automatic right of entry without a warrant.

If the police or Gambling Commission have reasonable grounds for suspecting an offence has been committed or that evidence of an offence may be found, under section 306 they may make an application to the magistrates' court for a warrant. The magistrates must satisfy themselves that one of the following is satisfied:

(a)   admission to the premises has been refused;

(b)   admission to the premises is likely to be refused unless a warrant is issued;

(c)   the purpose of entry may be frustrated or prejudiced if immediate entry cannot be secured; and

(d)   there is likely to be no-one present to grant admission.

The power under section 306 cannot be carried out by local authority authorised persons.

Inspection of gambling

A constable, enforcement officer or authorised person has the power to enter premises if it is reasonably suspected that facilities for gambling are being, are about to be or have been, provided on the premises. This does not apply if the suspected gambling is private or non-commercial gaming or betting. (Section 307.)

Operating licence holders

A constable or enforcement officer has the power to enter premises reasonably believed to be in use by the holder of an operating licence partly or entirely for purposes connected with the licensed activities, to determine whether the terms and conditions of the operating licence are being met (section 308).

Family entertainment centres

If an application is received for a family entertainment centre and gaming machine permit, officers of all enforcement agencies have a right of entry. If the permit is granted, the same people have powers of entry. (Section 309.)

Premises licensed for alcohol

If an application is made for a licensed premises gaming machine permit, enforcement officers or authorised persons have a right of entry. Police constables, enforcement officers and authorised persons can enter premises which hold an on-premises licence under the Licensing Act 2003 to check the number of machines and their category, whether or not any gaming taking place complies with the relevant regulations, and whether or not any games of bingo being played comply with statutory requirements. (Section 310.)

Prize gaming permit

Where applications are made for a prize gaming permit, all the enforcement agencies have a right of entry. If a permit is granted, they have similar powers of entry. (Section 311.)

Clubs

Where an application is made for a club gaming permit or club machine permit, authorised persons have a right of entry to the premises which is the subject of the application. Police constables and enforcement officers have rights of entry to clubs at any time. The right of entry for these two agencies is the right to check whether gaming is taking place on the premises and, if it is, whether it complies with relevant regulations, club gaming permit or club machine permit. (Section 312.)

Licensed premises

Where an application is made for a premises licence or an application is received to review such a licence, police constables, enforcement officers and authorised persons have a right of entry (section 313).

Lotteries: registered societies

Enforcement officers and authorised persons have a right to enter any premises owned or used by a society registered with a local authority for the purpose of making any enquiries about a lottery promoted by that society (section 314).

Temporary use notice

If a temporary use notice is served, all the enforcement agencies have a right of entry to assess the likely effect of the premises being used for gambling, in the light of the licensing objectives. If no representations are received to the temporary use notice and it has effect, all the agencies have a right of entry to the premises while the notice has effect. (Section 315.)

Dwellings

Persons exercising a power of entry under the Act may only enter a dwelling where authorised to do so by warrant (section 318).

Authorisations: production on demand

Section 316 allows a constable or enforcement officer to require an operating licence holder who has given a written authorisation, or the person to whom the authorisation has been given, to produce a copy of the authorisation. Failure to comply, without reasonable excuse, is an offence. The maximum penalty for the offence is a fine not exceeding level 2 on the standard scale.

The types of authorisation which can be demanded under this section are:

1.   In relation to a pool betting operating licence, where the licence holder has authorised a person to accept bets on his behalf on a horserace course or dog track.

2.   In relation to a pool betting operating licence which authorises the provision of facilities for football pools, where the licence holder has authorised a person to receive payments or entries on his behalf.

3.   In relation to a pool betting operating licence which authorises horserace pool betting, where the licence

holder has authorised a person to provide facilities for horserace pool betting.

4.   In relation to a casino premises licence, where the licence holder has authorised a person or persons to use the premises for providing betting, bingo or both.

Entry of premises for inspection

Powers upon entry

Police constables, enforcement officers and authorised persons have certain powers when entering premises under section 317 of the Act.

These powers include the right to inspect any part of the premises and any machine or other thing on them, question any person on the premises, access any written or electronic record on the premises and request copies. They also have the right to seize and retain material, but only where the person entering believes that it contains or constitutes evidence of an offence under the Act or a breach of licence conditions. The Secretary of State has the power to make regulations concerning the treatment of copies of written or electronic records supplied and items removed as evidence of an offence (past or present) or breach of licence conditions. Regulations may also include provisions regarding the retention, use, return or destruction of items supplied or removed and the conferring of a right of appeal.

Restrictions are imposed on the extent to which a person entering premises can have access to and seize records without a warrant. It is only where a record (whether written or electronic) relates entirely to the matters to which the power of entry relates that it can be accessed or seized without a warrant.

It should be noted that, when carrying out powers under section 317, the provisions of the Police and Criminal Evidence Act 1984 and any relevant codes of practice must be followed.

Records

Section 319 provides that a person entering under Part 15 may only inspect or seize records (whether written or electronic) without a warrant where the records relate entirely to the matters to which the power of entry relates. Where records also contain information which is not relevant to those matters (i.e. where they are "mixed" records), they may only be inspected or seized under the powers in paragraphs (c) to (e) of section 317(1) under the authority of a warrant.

Timing

A power of entry can only be exercised at a reasonable time. What is a "reasonable time" will depend on the circumstances of each case. (Section 320.)

Evidence of authorisation

An enforcement officer or authorised person wishing to exercise a power of entry under the Act is required to produce evidence of identity and authority to a person (if there is one) who appears to be occupying the premises or to have responsibility for their management (section 321).

Information

Section 322 requires the Secretary of State to make regulations about the information to be provided by those entering premises in reliance on a power under the Act. The regulations are to make provision about the nature of the information to be provided. They are also to prescribe the form and manner in which the information is to be provided, the person to whom it is to be provided and the timing of its provision. Subsection (3) imposes a duty on a constable, enforcement officer or authorised person exercising a power of entry to comply with any relevant provision of regulations made under this section. The current regulations are the Gambling Act 2005 (Inspection) (Provision of Information) Regulations 2007 (see page 149).

Use of force

A constable has the authority to use reasonable force to enter premises when exercising powers under the Act. An enforcement officer has the authority to use reasonable force to enter premises where the entry is because he suspects that an offence under the Act has been, is being or is about to be committed on the premises. An authorised person or enforcement officer has the authority to use reasonable force to enter premises if he suspects that gambling (other than private or non-commercial gaming or betting) is taking place. (Section 323.)

Person accompanying inspector, etc.

Section 324 allows a constable, enforcement officer or authorised person to be accompanied by others when exercising a power to enter premises under the Act.

Securing premises after entry

A constable, enforcement officer or authorised person who enters premises is required to take reasonable steps to ensure that the premises remain as secure as they were when they entered (section 325).

Obstruction

Section 326 makes it an offence to obstruct or fail to co-operate with a constable, enforcement officer or authorised person exercising a power of entry. For example, it will be an offence to block the doorway to premises where an enforcement officer has requested entry. The maximum penalty for the offence is a fine not exceeding level 3 on the standard scale.

The Gambling Act 2005 (Inspection) (Provision of Information) Regulations 2007

The Secretary of State has made regulations under section 322 of the Gambling Act 2005 regarding steps to be taken by inspectors carrying out an inspection under the Act.

An inspector means a constable, enforcement officer or authorised person.

The Regulations also use the phrase "interested person". This means:

(a) the Gambling Commission;

(b) an appropriate recipient;

(c) the holder of a premises licence or permit;

(d) a person who served a temporary use notice;

(e) a small lottery society registered with the Licensing Authority;

(f) anyone who occupies the premises or is responsible for their management at the time of the inspection.

"Appropriate recipient" means a person present at the premises at any time during an inspection and who appears to the inspector to occupy the premises or to be responsible for their management.

Where any inspector enters premises, they must produce their authorisation and ensure that anyone who accompanies them produces evidence of their identity.

The inspector must make the appropriate recipient aware, either orally or in writing:

(a) that following the inspection they may make a request in writing for the inspector to provide a written report of the inspection;

(b) of the manner in which such a request can be made; and

(c) who is entitled to a copy of the written report.

The notice the inspector has to provide must include the following:

1. The postal address of the premises.

2. The name of the inspector who visited the premises and the name of any person accompanying him.

3. The date and time when the inspector entered the premises.

4. A description of the power that the inspector exercised to enter the premises, together with a reference to the relevant section of the Act.

5. A record of any part of the premises, or any machine or other thing on the premises, that was inspected in exercise of the inspector's power under section 317(1)(a).

6. A record of any written or electronic record to which the inspector required access under section 317(1)(c).

7. A description of any copies of written or electronic records that were supplied to the inspector in compliance with his request under section 317(1)(d), specifying the form in which they were supplied.

8. A record of anything that was removed from the premises and the reasons for its removal.

9. A record of whether any force was used for the purpose of entering the premises, by whom it was used and the reason why it was used.

10. If force was used for the purpose of entering the premises, a record of what steps were taken in accordance with section 325, to ensure that when the inspector left the premises they were as secure as they were before he entered.

11. A record of any damage caused during the inspection, and of the circumstances in which it was caused.

If at no time during the visit the appropriate recipient is present, the inspector must leave a written notice setting out:

(a) the fact that the premises have been inspected;

(b) the name of any inspector who carried out the inspection;

(c) the date of the inspection; and

(d) the fact that they are entitled to a written record of the inspection and how this request may be made.

If at any time an inspector puts a question to a person on the premises and that person refuses to answer the question, the inspector must orally inform the person they are exercising their power to question under section 317(1)(b) and that it is an offence if, without reasonable excuse, the person obstructs or fails to co-operate with the inspector.

PROTECTION OF CHILDREN AND YOUNG PERSONS

Part 4 of the Gambling Act 2005 sets out a number of offences relating to children and young persons being involved in any form of gambling.

Meaning of child and young person

A child is someone below the age of 16 years. Someone 16 or 17 years of age is a young person. (Section 45.)

Inviting children and young persons to gamble; participation by young persons in gambling

It is an offence to invite children or young persons to gamble (section 46). Section 48 provides that a young person commits an offence if they gamble. This does not apply, however, to private or non-commercial gambling using Category D gaming machines and the equal chance gaming at family entertainment centres.

The offence of inviting people to gamble includes advertising.

Invitation to enter premises; young persons entering premises

An offence is committed by inviting or permitting someone below the age of 18 years to enter premises such as a casino, betting shop or adult gaming centre (section 47).

Children and young persons can enter bingo premises and the betting areas of racecourses when races are being held.

Provision of facilities for gambling

A young person commits an offence if they provide facilities for gambling. However, this does not apply in respect of private or non-commercial gambling, lotteries, football pools or equal chance prize gaming which is provided at a travelling fair. (Section 50.)

Employment of children and young persons in gambling

Section 51 creates the offence of employing anyone below the age of 18 to provide facilities for gambling unless it is in connection with private or non-commercial gambling, lotteries, football pools or equal chance prize gaming at a travelling fair.

Under section 52 it is an offence for a child to be employed in connection with providing facilities for a lottery or football pools.

If a child is employed to provide any function when bingo is being played, or gambling is being played in connection with the benefit of a club gaming permit or club machine permit, an offence is committed under section 53.

Invitation to participate in lottery

An offence is committed if anyone invites, causes or permits a child to take part in a lottery. No offence is committed however, if the lottery is a private lottery or a non-commercial lottery. (Section 56.)

Invitation to participate in football pools

No-one can invite, cause or permit a child to take part in football pools. If they do, an offence is committed under section 57.

Return of stake

Section 83 provides that all operating licences contain a condition that, if a licensee becomes aware that someone below the age of 18 is using or has used their facilities for gambling, they must return the money staked and cannot pay any winnings. If the stake is not returned, an offence is committed under section 58.

Age limit for Category D machines

Section 59 enables the Secretary of State to make regulations setting a minimum age limit below which a child or young person cannot use a Category D machine. If any regulations are made, it will become an offence to invite, cause or permit someone below the age of the specified age limit to use Category D machines. No regulations had been made at the time of publication of this book.

Temporary use notice

If a temporary use notice or an occasional use notice has been served and the activity authorised under the notice is taking place, then the part of the premises where the gaming is being held is to be regarded as if a relevant premises licence is in force. The effect of this is that no-one below the age of 18 can enter the part of the premises where a temporary use notice or occasional use notice is in force. (Section 60.)

Penalty

Anyone convicted of one of the above offences can be jailed for 51 weeks and/or fined a maximum fine of level 5. If the offences are committed by a young person, on conviction they can only be fined up to a maximum fine of level 3. (Section 62.)

Reasonable belief about a person's age

Section 63 provides a defence to a prosecution, if the person charged proves:

(a) they took all reasonable steps to determine the individual's age; and

(b) they reasonably believed the individual was not a child or a young person.

Use of children in enforcement operations

Test purchases are lawful under the Gambling Act 2005. Section 64 makes it clear that no offence of inviting a child or a young person to gamble is committed if they are requested to do so by a police constable, enforcement officer or authorised person.

Prosecution

The principal powers to prosecute for offences in respect of children and young persons lie with the police and the Gambling Commission. Section 346 of the Gambling Act 2005 sets out the offences where the Licensing Authority may institute criminal proceedings. However, section 346(2) states that the section is "without prejudice to section 222 of the Local Government Act 1972". This seems to indicate that, if the Licensing Authority do not have a specific power to prosecute for an offence under the Act but they consider it is in the interests of the residents of their area to do so, they may commence proceedings.

GRANDFATHER RIGHTS

Grandfather rights for businesses requiring premises licences expired on 31 August 2007. However, for clubs and public houses no applications need to be made until the authorisation under the previous legislation expires.

The only caveat to this is that, if a public house or club has a current authorisation which expires after 31 August 2010, the application under the Gambling Act 2005 will have to be made prior to that date.

Clubs and Miners' Welfare Institutes registered under the Gaming Act 1968 are entitled to a club gaming or club machine permit. There is a fast track procedure for clubs holding grandfather rights. The effect of this is that no representations can be made to the application for a permit.

OFFENCES UNDER THE GAMBLING ACT 2005

Offence	Section
Providing facilities for gambling (unless authorised by an operating licence and carried on in accordance with terms and conditions – or otherwise permitted under the Act).	s.33
Using premises, or causing or permitting them to be used, to: (a) operate a casino; (b) provide facilities to play bingo; (c) make a gaming machine available for use; (d) provide other facilities for gaming; or (e) provide facilities for betting (unless authorised by a premises licence or otherwise permitted under the Act).	s.37
Manufacturing, supplying, installing or adapting gambling software (unless authorised by an operating licence).	s.41
Cheating at gambling, or assisting or enabling another to cheat.	s.42
Inviting another to join, or knowingly participating in the administration, promotion or management of, a chain-gift scheme.	s.43
Doing anything in Great Britain, including using remote gambling equipment located in Great Britain, for the purpose of inviting or enabling a person in a prohibited territory to participate in remote gambling.	s.44
Inviting, causing or permitting a person under 18 to gamble (unless otherwise permitted under the Act).	s.46
Inviting or permitting a child or young person to enter a casino, betting shop or adult gaming centre when facilities for gambling are being provided (unless otherwise permitted under the Act).	s.47

Offence	Section
Inviting or permitting a child or young person to enter areas of a track where facilities for betting are provided or where gaming machines (other than Category D machines) are situated, when racing is not taking place.	s.47
A young person gambling (unless otherwise permitted under the Act).	s.48
A young person entering gambling premises (unless otherwise permitted under the Act).	s.49
A young person providing facilities for gambling (unless otherwise permitted under the Act).	s.50
Employing a child or young person to provide facilities for gambling or to work in premises where facilities for gambling are provided (unless otherwise permitted under the Act).	s.51-s.55
Inviting, causing or permitting a child to take part in a lottery (unless otherwise permitted under the Act).	s.56
Inviting, causing, or permitting a child to participate in football pools.	s.57
Failing to return any stakes paid by children or young people not permitted to participate in the gambling activity.	s.58
Making a gaming machine available for use (unless otherwise permitted under the Act).	s.242
Making available for use a "linked" gaming machine (unless otherwise permitted under the Act).	s.244
Supplying, installing or making available for use a gaming machine that accepts payments by credit card.	s.245
Manufacturing, supplying, installing, maintaining or repairing a gaming machine or part of a gaming machine, unless: (a) this is done in accordance with an operating licence; (b) the machine is used in circumstances in which users do not acquire the opportunity to win a prize; or (c) this is done under a permit issued by the Gambling Commission for not less than one year limited to a specific machine.	s.243, s.248, s.250

Offence	Section
Promoting a lottery, unless: (a) this is done in accordance with an operating licence; (b) this is done on behalf of an operating licence holder, and in accordance with the terms of the licence; or (c) it is an exempt lottery.	s.258
Facilitating a lottery, unless this is done in accordance with an operating licence or it is an exempt lottery.	s.259
Misusing any part of the profits of a lottery; misusing any part of the profits of an exempt lottery.	s.260, s.261
In the case of a small society lottery: (a) promoting a lottery at a time when the society concerned is not registered with a local authority; (b) failing to comply with the Act's requirements for filing records; or (c) · providing false or misleading information in connection with the filing of records.	s.262
Using or permitting the use of any part of the profits of non-commercial gaming (or non-commercial equal chance gaming) for any purpose other than the fundraising purpose specified by the organiser.	s.302
Breaching the regulations on advertising gambling.	s.328
Advertising unlawful gambling.	s.330
Advertising foreign gambling.	s.331
Giving false or misleading information to the Gambling Commission or a Licensing Authority for a purpose connected with a provision of the Act.	s.342

Offences for which the Licensing Authority has specific power to prosecute

Offence	Section
Operating without a premises licence.	s.37
Failing to keep the premises licence on the premises or making it available to a police constable, an enforcement officer or an authorised officer of the Licensing Authority.	s.185
The holder of a premises licence failing to notify the Licensing Authority as soon as reasonably practicable of a change of home or business address.	s.186
Failing to display prominently a temporary use notice and failing to produce the notice endorsed by the Licensing Authority to a constable, an officer of HM Revenue and Customs, an enforcement officer or an authorised officer of the Licensing Authority.	s.229
Making a gaming machine available for use unless there is an operating licence or appropriate permit in force or making a gaming machine available for use in contravention of any regulations made by the Secretary of State in respect of the use of such machines.	s.242
Promoting a lottery unless there is an operating licence in force or it is an exempt lottery.	s.258
Facilitating a lottery (e.g. printing tickets) unless acting in accordance with the terms and conditions of an operating licence or the lottery is an exempt lottery.	s.259
Misusing the profits of a lottery.	s.260
Misusing the profits of an exempt lottery.	s.261
A non-commercial lottery commits an offence if it promotes a lottery when it is not registered with the local authority or it fails to comply with any of the statutory requirements or provides false or misleading information.	s.262
Obstructing an authorised person exercising their powers under the legislation.	s.326
Giving false information in connection with any application under the Act.	s.342

Offence	*Schedule*
Failing to produce a permit when so requested by a police constable, an enforcement officer or an authorised officer of the Licensing Authority. Failing to produce a family entertainment centre gaming machine permit when so requested by a constable, an enforcement officer or an authorised officer of the Licensing Authority.	Sch 10, para 20
Failing to produce a licensed premises gaming machine permit when requested by a constable, an enforcement officer or an authorised officer of the Licensing Authority.	Sch 13, para 10
Failing to produce a prize gaming permit when so requested by a constable, an enforcement officer or an authorised officer of the Licensing Authority.	Sch 14, para 20

APPENDIX OF FORMS

The following forms are all available from Shaw & Sons Limited as paper copy or via the Shaw's Forms on Disk service. For full details, telephone 01322 621100.

Part 8 – Premises Licences	
GA151TC	Summary of the terms and conditions of a Premises Licence
GA159	Application for a Premises Licence under the Gambling Act 2005 (standard form)
GA159V	Application for a Premises Licence under the Gambling Act 2005 (vessel)
GA159TC	Application for a Premises Licence under the Gambling Act 2005 (transitional conversion application)
GA159TCV	Application for a Premises Licence under the Gambling Act 2005 (transitional conversion application) (vessel)
GA160	Notice of Application for a Premises Licence (to be given to responsible authorities) (one applicant)
GA160P	Notice of Application for a Premises Licence under the Gambling Act 2005 (Notice to be published)
GA160X	Notice of Application for a Premises Licence (to be given to responsible authorities) (two or more applicants)
GA162(3)	Notice by licensing authority of proposal to determine application for Premises Licence due to representations if a vexatious or frivolous nature etc
GA162	Notice of hearing [of representations] in respect of application for Premises Licence
GA164	Premises Licence
GA164G	Notice of grant of an application for a Premises Licence
GAGA-A	ANNEX A – Conditions to be attached (grant of application under Part 8)
GAGA-B	ANNEX B – Conditions to be excluded (grant of application under Part 8)

GAGA-C	ANNEX C – Representations (grant of applications under Part 8)
GA165	Notice of rejection of application for a Premises Licence
GA187	Application to vary a Premises Licence under the Gambling Act 2005
GA187(3)	Notice of hearing [of representations] in respect of application to vary Premises Licence
GA187G	Notice of grant of an application to vary a Premises Licence
GA187N	Notice of application to vary a Premises Licence (to be given to the responsible authorities) (one applicant only)
GA187N-P	Notice of application to vary a Premises Licence under the Gambling Act 2005 (Notice to be published)
GA187N-X	Notice of application to vary a Premises Licence (to be given to the responsible authorities) (two or more applicants)
GA187R	Notice of rejection of an application to vary a Premises Licence
GA188	Application to transfer a Premises Licence under the Gambling Act 2005
GA188(3)	Notice of hearing [of representations] in respect of application to transfer Premises Licence
GA188G	Notice of grant of a application to transfer a Premises Licence
GA188N	Notice of application to transfer a Premises Licence (to be given to the responsible authorities) (one applicant only)
GA188N-X	Notice of application to transfer a Premises Licence (to be given to the responsible authorities) (two or more applicants)
GA188R	Notice of rejection of an application to transfer a Premises Licence
GA189(1)(a)	Notice to a licensee of Premises Licence that Licensing Authority will disapply section 188(3)(b)

GA189(1)(b)	Notice to applicant of determination by Licensing Authority not to disapply section 188(3)(b)
GA190	Application for copy of [Premises Licence issued] [summary given] under section 164
GA192	Notice of surrender of Premises Licence
GA193	Notice of revocation of Premises Licence due to failure to pay annual fee
GA195	Application for the reinstatement of a Premises Licence under the Gambling Act 2005
GA195-6	Notice of hearing [of representations] in respect of application for reinstatement of Premises Licence
GA195G	Notice of grant of an application for the reinstatement of a Premises Licence
GA195N	Notice of grant of an application for the reinstatement of a Premises Licence (to be given to the responsible authorities) (one applicant only)
GA195N-X	Notice of grant of an application for the reinstatement of a Premises Licence (to be given to the responsible authorities) (two or more applicants)
GA195R	Notice of rejection of an application for reinstatement of a Premises Licence
GA197	Application for a review of a Premises Licence under the Gambling Act 2005
GA197(3)	Notice of application for a review of a Premises Licence
G197(4)	Notice of application for a review of a Premises Licence under the Gambling Act 2005
GA200(3)(a)	Notice of intention to hold a review of a Premises Licence
GA200(3)(b)	Notice of intention to hold a review of a Premises Licence under the Gambling Act 2005 (publishing)
GA201	Notice of hearing to consider [Local Authority intention to] [an application for] review of premises licence and any relative representations
GA204	Application for a provisional statement under the Gambling Act 2005 (standard form)
GA204G	Notice of grant of an application for a Provisional Statement

GA204H	Notice of hearing [of representations] regarding application for Provisional Statement in respect of premises
GA204N	Notice of application for a Provisional Statement (to be given to the responsible authorities) (one applicant only)
GA204N-P	Notice of application for a Provisional Statement under the Gambling Act 2005 (Notice to be published)
GA204N-X	Notice of application for a Provisional Statement (to be given to the responsible authorities) (two or more applicants)
GA204PS	Provisional Statement
GA204R	Notice of rejection of an application for a Provisional Statement
GA204V	Application for a Provisional Statement under the Gambling Act 2005 (vessel)
GAR1	Notice of actions following receipt of notice of hearing
Part 9 – Temporary Use of Premises	
GA220	Acknowledgement of notice
GA221	Notice of objection
GA222	Notice of hearing of representations about notice of objection
GA225	Dismissal of objection
GA227(6)	Application for copy of endorsed copy of a temporary use notice [lost][stole][damaged]
GA230	Notice of withdrawal of temporary use notice
Part 12 – Clubs, Pubs, Fairs	
GA284	Order disapplying section [279][282(1)] of the Gambling Act 2005
GA284(1)	Notification of making order under section 284(1)
GA28(3)	Notice of intention to make order to disapply section [279] [282(1)]
GA284(3)(c)	Notice of hearing to hear representations with respect to intention to make an order to disapply section [279][282(1)]

Part 15 – Inspection	
GA306	Application for warrant to enter premises under section 306 of the Gambling Act 2005
GA306(2)	Warrant to enter and search premises
GA306(4)	Notice of intention to apply for warrant to enter premises
GA318	Application for warrant to enter dwelling under section 318 of the Gambling Act 2005
GA318(2)	Warrant to enter and search dwelling
GA318(4)	Notice of intention to apply for warrant to enter dwelling
GA322S	Statement on Entry
GA322W	Written record of inspection
Schedule 10 – Family Entertainment Centre Gaming Machine Permits	
GA10p8	Family Entertainment Centre Gaming Machine Permit
GA10p8(3)	Notice of grant of application for [renewal of] Family Entertainment Centre Gaming Machine Permit
GA10p8(4)a	Notice of refusal of application for Family Entertainment Centre Gaming Machine Permit
GA10p10	Notice of intention to refuse the application for [the renewal of] a Family Entertainment Centre Gaming Machine Permit
GA10p11(2)aii	Request that a new name be substituted for old name on Family Entertainment Centre Gaming Machine Permit
GA10p14	Notification that premises are not being used as a Family Entertainment Centre
GA10p15(1)b	Notification that permit holder has become incapable of carrying on authorised activities
GA10p16	Notice of surrender of Family Entertainment Centre Gaming Machine Permit
GA10p18(4)	Notice of refusal of application for renewal of Family Entertainment Centre Gaming Machine Permit

GA10p21	Application for copy of Family Entertainment Centre Gaming Machine Permit which has been [lost][stolen][damaged]
Schedule 11 – Exempt Lotteries	
GA11p42	Application form for Registration of Non-Commercial Society
GA11p44	Notification of society registration
GA11p49	Notice of intent to refuse application to register society
GA11p47	Notification of refusal of application for registration for society
GA11p50(3)	Notice of intent to revoke registration
GA11p50	Notice of revocation for society registration
GA11p52	Application for registration cancellation
GA11p53	Notice of registration cancellation for society
GA11p54	Notice of registration cancellation for society due to failure to pay annual fee
Schedule 12 – Club Gaming Permits and Club Machine Permits	
GA12p2	Application Form for Club Gaming Permit or Club Machine Permit
GA12p7	Notice of [decision to dispense with] hearing on objections to application [renewal of] for [club gaming permit] [club machine permit]
GA12p8	Notice granting application for [renewal of] [club gaming permit] [club machine permit]
GA12p9	Notice refusing application for renewal of] [club gaming permit] [club machine permit]
GA12p11G	Club Gaming Permit
GA12p11M	Club Machine Permit
GA12p15	Application to vary [club gaming permit] [club machine permit]
GA12p15(3)	Notice of decision to vary [club gaming permit] [club machine permit]
GA12p15(4)	Notice of decision to refuse application to vary a [club gaming permit] [club machine permit]

GA12p15(5)	Notice of hearing on application to vary [club gaming permit] [club machine permit]
GA12p16	Application for certified copy of [club gaming permit] [club machine permit]
GA12p16(4)	Grant and issue of certified copy of [club gaming permit][club machine permit]
GA12p19	Notice of surrender of [club gaming permit] [club machine permit]
Schedule 13 – Licensed Premises Gaming Machine Permits	
GA13p7	Licensed Premises Gaming Machine Permit
GA13p7(2)	Notice by permit holder of name change
GA13p11	Application for copy of Licensed Premises Gaming Machine Permit
GA13p11(4)	Grant and issue of certified copy of Licensed Premises Gaming Machine Permit
GA13p4(2)(G)	Notice granting application for a Licensed Premises Gaming Machine Permit
GA13p5(3)	Notice refusing application for a Licensed Premises Gaming Machine Permit
Ga13p6G	Notice of intent to grant application for a Licensed Premises Gaming Machine Permit [for a [smaller number of machines][different category of machines][smaller number of machines and a different category of machines]]
GA13p6R	Notice of intent to refuse application for a Licensed Premises Gaming Machine Permit
GA13p14	Notice of surrender of Licensed Premises Gaming Machine Permit
GA13p17	Notice cancelling Licensed Premises Gaming Machine Permit due to failure to pay annual fee
Schedule 14 – Prize Gaming Permits	
GA14p11	Notice of intention to refuse the application for [the renewal of] a Prize Gaming Permit
GA14p9	Prize Gaming Permit
GA14p9(3)	Notice of grant of application for [renewal of] Prize Gaming Permit

GA14p9(4)a	Notice of refusal of application for [renewal of] Prize Gaming Permit
GA14p12(2)aii	Request that a new name be substituted for old name on Prize Gaming Permit
GA14p15(1)b	Notification that Prize Gaming Permit holder has become incapable of carrying on authorized activities
GA14p16	Notice of surrender of Prize Gaming Permit
GA14p21	Application for copy of Prize Gaming Permit which has been [lost][stolen][damaged]

INDEX